GOLF
FACTS

GOLF
FACTS

Ian Morrison

BARNES
&NOBLE
BOOKS
NEW YORK

A QUANTUM BOOK

This hardback edition published
by Barnes & Noble, Inc.,
by arrangement with Quantum Books Ltd
1997 Barnes & Noble Books

Copyright © 1993 Quarto Publishing plc

ISBN 1-55619-082-7

QUMGOF

M   10   9   8   7   6   5   4   3

This book was produced by
Quantum Books Ltd
6 Blundell Street
London N7 9BH

Senior Editor Honor Head

American Editor Maggie McCormick

Art Editor Philip Gilderdale

Designer Anne Fisher

Illustrator Maps Janos Marffy

Diagrams Kuo Kang Chen

Cartoons Ross Thomson

Picture Manager Rebecca Horsewood

Picture Researcher Mandy Little

Art Director Moira Clinch

Publishing Director Janet Slingsby

Quarto would like to thank the following for their
assistance: Mr. Livingstone, South Herts
Golf Club, London, England and Wilson
Sporting Goods Ltd.

Typeset by En to En Typesetting
Manufactured in Hong Kong by
Regent Publishing Services Ltd.
Printed in Singapore by Star Standard Industries Pte. Ltd

Captions for the pictures on the opening pages at the
beginning of each chapter are as follows: **page 6** Walter
Hagen; **page 7** Early golf ball; **page 16** Jack Nicklaus ;
page 42 Nick Price; **page 43** Joyce Wethered; **page 82**
An aerial view of the Pinehurst Golf course in the USA.

CONTENTS

HOW IT ALL STARTED 6

PLAYING THE GAME 16

GOLF GREATS 42

OUTSTANDING GOLF COURSES 82

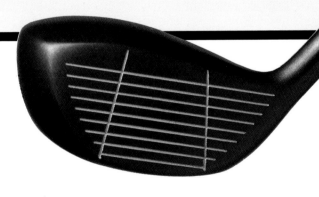

How It All Started

HISTORIANS HAVE BEEN trying to unravel the origin of golf for years, and the definitive answer has not yet been found. If you think about it logically, we could have been playing golf in prehistoric times. It needed only a stick to use as a club and a stone as a ball and - wow! - we had golf. But many sports can be said to have derived from such ancient origins, so let's look at the realistic claims to golf's origins . . .

A HISTORY OF THE GAME

A STAINED-GLASS window installed in Gloucester Cathedral in England in the mid-14th century depicts a man swinging a stick at a ball. The window was commissioned by Sir Thomas Broadstone, but nothing more is known about the game being played by the man in the window. It could have been *cambuca*, which was a popular stick-and-ball game of the day.

About the same time, in 1353, there was a popular stick-and-ball game in Flanders. The object was to hit the ball across undulating terrain toward a predetermined goal such as a tree or gate, etc. This game was called *chole* and certainly bore a resemblance to the modern-day game of golf. So, did the Belgians invent the game? The Dutch also had a similar game called *kolfspel*. Are *they* therefore responsible for giving us golf?

The Scots were certainly playing the game in the 15th century because, in 1457, the first of three Acts of Parliament banning *gouf* was passed. They probably had been playing the game for some time before the ban; otherwise, playing it would hardly have aroused disapproval. Like soccer, which had been banned thirty years earlier, *gouf* was taking the

Above A pair of 14th century "Golfers".

Right A detail of the window in England's Gloucester Cathedral.

Below The entire East Window at Gloucester Cathedral, which was installed in the mid-14th century.

GOLF'S SPORTING QUEEN

Mary, Queen of Scots, became queen of Scotland when she was only six days old, in 1542. She was 25 when she abdicated, but in that time she had caused quite a stir on both sides of the border and posed a threat to England's Queen, Elizabeth I. She had also become an avid golfer. Furthermore, she was a billiards fan, and when she was held prisoner by Elizabeth I, she is said to have demanded that a billiard table be installed in her cell.

Mary's second husband was her cousin Henry Stuart, Lord Darnley, but he was murdered in 1567, blown up by gunpowder. Within two weeks of his assassination, Mary was out on the golf links at Seton House, where she played regularly. Her behavior fueled the belief that she had arranged his killing to end their stormy two-year marriage. Mary was herself executed in 1587.

able-bodied men of Scotland away from their much-needed archery practice. Further Acts banned *gouf* in 1470 and 1491. The last was passed by King James IV, but ten years later it is recorded that he bought himself a set of golf clubs!

The birthright of golf has, therefore, not been precisely established. But one thing is certain: Scotland is the "home" of golf, and it was from there that the game spread to become one of the most international of all sports.

The Archbishop of St. Andrews gave his approval for the people of the Burgh to play golf over the local links in 1553, and fourteen years later Mary, Queen of Scots became one of golf's best-known exponents.

Royalty and nobility were soon followed as golfing enthusiasts by other members of the community, and in a short time links were being developed all over Scotland. With golf's increased popularity came the need for organized clubs and, of course, the inevitable set of rules.

JOINING THE CLUB

THE FIRST GOLF CLUB, the Edinburgh Golfing Society, later the Royal Burgess Golfing Society of Edinburgh, was founded in 1735, nine years before the formation of the Gentlemen Golfers of Edinburgh (later the Honourable Company of Edinburgh Golfers), who were responsible for drawing up golf's first set of rules - 13 of them.

Ten years after the Honourable Company's birth, the St. Andrews Club (later the Royal and Ancient) was formed, and its original set of rules was almost identical to the Honourable Company's.

While the rules had become standardized, the number of holes had not. The Honourable Company's original links in Leith consisted of five holes, while St. Andrews' original course had 12 greens and a total of 22 holes. It was reduced to 18 holes in 1764; and, because of St. Andrews' stature, other clubs eventually followed suit, either extending or reducing their courses to 18 holes.

While it is recorded that the Prince of Wales played golf at Greenwich around 1608, the sport's rapid spread south to England came in the latter half of the 18th century following the formation of the

THE WORLD'S OLDEST GOLF CLUBS

1735 Royal Burgess Golfing Society of Edinburgh (a)
1744 Honourable Company of Edinburgh Golfers
1754 Royal and Ancient (St. Andrews)
1761 Bruntsfield Links Golfing Society
1766 Royal Blackheath (b)
1774 Royal Musselburgh
1780 Royal Aberdeen
1787 Glasgow Gailes
1787 Glasgow Killermont
1791 Cruden Bay (Aberdeenshire)

(a) The Royal Burgess Golfing Society of Edinburgh is credited with being formed in 1735 as the Edinburgh Golf Society, and did not assume the title of Edinburgh Burgess until 1787. Most sources accept that the oldest golf club in the world is therefore the Honourable Company of Edinburgh Golfers.

(b) The exact date of the formation of the Blackheath Club is uncertain, and some sources record that golf was played there in the 17th century by King James VI of Scotland. But it is generally accepted that the club was formed in 1766.

Left Four gentlemen golfers, with their caddies, playing at the St. Andrews links in 1798. Note how the four players are dressed alike, as are the caddies.

first English Club, Royal Blackheath, in 1766.

As Britons set sail for other continents, many of them took their bag of golf clubs with them and spread the golfing word. The Calcutta Club in India (later the Royal Calcutta Club) became the first organized club outside Britain in 1829, and in 1856 the Pau club in France became the first on the mainland of Europe.

From there, the sport spread rapidly, and by the turn of the century it was being played in many corners of the globe.

Australia's first club, the Adelaide, was formed in 1870. New Zealand had its first organized club at Dunedin a year later, and inevitably the sport found its way to North America, where the Montreal Club was formed in 1873.

Perhaps surprisingly, early attempts to develop the game in the United States had failed. The Crail Golfing Society in South Carolina was formed in 1786, but it did not last. Neither did the Oakhurst Club in Virginia, which was formed in 1884. However, four years later, golf "arrived" in the USA when the St. Andrews Club in Yonkers, New York, was formed. In 1894 the United States Golf Association was founded and remains the ruling body for the game in North America.

Like many other nations, the USA inaugurated its own Championships, following the lead of the Prestwick Club, which started the British Open Championship in 1860.

DID YOU KNOW?

The first book about golf was The Golfer's Manual published in 1857. Its author, H. B. Farnie, used the penname "A Keen Hand."

THE HONOURABLE COMPANY

The Society of the Gentlemen Golfers of Edinburgh was formed on May 1, 1744, under their first president Duncan Forbes of Culloden. There is evidence to suggest that golf had been played over five holes at the Leith links before that date, but 1744 is when they are officially credited with forming their Society. In that year the Provost of Edinburgh donated a splendid silver golf club as a trophy to be contested annually. It remains one of the most cherished of all golfing trophies. Not only did the annual winner receive the silver trophy, but he was also designated the "captain of the club" and was responsible for resolving all golfing disputes among the members. Consequently, the Gentlemen Golfers drew up the game's first set of rules.

In 1759 they were granted permission to adopt the title the Honourable Company of Edinburgh Golfers. Sadly, they ceased to exist in 1831. But after five years they were re-formed with Musselburgh as their new home. In 1891 they moved down the East Lothian coast to their present home at Muirfield and the following year the course was the site of the British Open for the first time.

EARLY TOOLS OF THE TRADE

THE PIONEERING GOLFERS of 200 years ago did not have the benefits of graphite-shafted clubs and other innovations that have developed to aid modern golfers. And they did not have skillfully manicured greens and well-cut fairways to play on. In the mid-1800s, there was no finer golfer than Young Tom Morris, but he never shot 18-hole rounds of 63 and 64, which the likes of Nick Faldo and Seve Ballesteros can do today with regularity.

Almost certainly, early golf clubs were made of wood. There is no documentary evidence to suggest what they were made of prior to the 18th century. But when the Honourable Company and the St. Andrews clubs were formed, all golf clubs were wooden, with hazel and ash the most popular for the shafts. Beech, apple, pear, or blackthorn were popular choices for the head, depending on whether

BAFFY, BRASSIE, AND MASHIE

Golf clubs in days gone by had some lovely names. Sadly, they are no longer with us, and they have been replaced by simple descriptions like 2-wood, 4-iron, wedge, and so on. The following list is of old clubs and their modern-day equivalents:

Old name	Current equivalent
Baffing Spoon (wood)	9-iron/wedge
Baffy	4-wood
Blaster	Sand wedge
Brassie	2-wood
Cleek	2-iron
Jigger (also known as a Sammy)	4-iron
Mashie	5-iron
Mashie-niblick	7-iron
Niblick	8/9-iron
Play Club	Driver
Spoon	3-wood

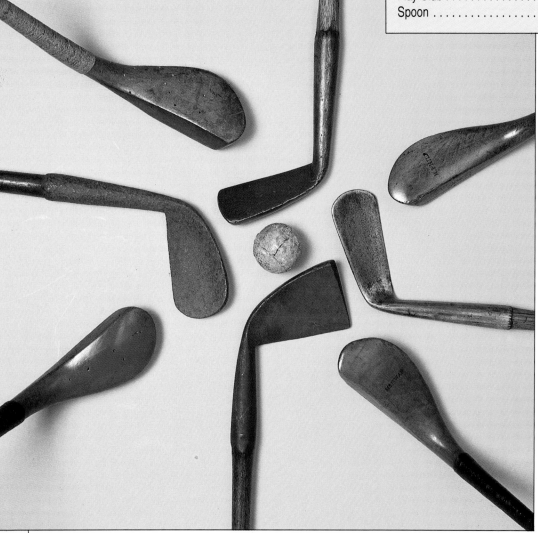

Left A selection of some early hickory-shafted clubs.

Right Major Boothby about to play a shot from close to the Swilcan Burn at St Andrews. Watching is Old Tom Morris (left) and Allan Robertson (on bridge with single club).

the club was for driving, playing fairway or approach shots, or putting. The head and shaft were glued together and bound with twine.

The day of the 14-club golfer was a long way off. Most top golfers would have five or six clubs at the most. But the top players soon realized there was a need to have a different club for each type of shot, and they soon started having clubs made with different lofts.

When the gutty ball arrived, it put a lot of strain on the club and it was then that iron-headed models gained in popularity. Hickory was used for the shafts instead of hazel or ash. By the end of the 19th century, club heads were becoming more standard in shape and size; top players used eight or nine clubs, and their caddies had special bags in which to carry them.

After the Haskell ball became popular, it was necessary to find another wood suitable for the wooden-headed clubs because the ball was causing damage to the traditional heads. North American persimmon was found to be ideal. However, damage was still being caused to the face of the club, and, consequently, ivory or bone inserts were added.

Because of the game's popularity, golf club manufacture was moving away from individual hand-made pieces of craftsmanship toward mass production; and when hickory was in short supply

after World War I, manufacturers turned to steel-shafted clubs, which were given the seal of approval by the US Professional Golf Association (USPGA) in 1924 and by the Royal & Ancient (R & A) in Scotland six years later.

Mass-produced clubs changed the shape of the game, as it was now possible to produce matched sets. For the first time a player was able to carry a set of matching clubs which differed only in length and loft. Weight, appearance, and feel of the club were the same, which led to a marked improvement in the standard of play among professionals and amateurs alike.

Modern golf clubs have seen persimmon wood replaced first by laminated plastic and subsequently by light aluminum heads, and steel shafts have made way for the more supple graphite and titanium ones. Single-piece clubs with the head and shaft working as a single unit give the golfer a closer relationship between club and ball. And cavity-back irons, with the backs hollowed out and with scientifically calculated centers of gravity to give a more controlled feel of the club, are essential to the 1990s golf professional - the day of the "game-improvement club" is upon us.

We have to wonder what Young Tom Morris could have achieved today with a bag of 1990s golf clubs.

THE DEVELOPMENT OF THE GOLF BALL

THE EARLIEST GOLF BALLS were carved out of wood. You can imagine how "round" they were! There were no such things as precision tools in those days. The first breakthrough in golf-ball manufacture came with the introduction of the "feathery," which was first seen in the 15th century. Each ball was made by stuffing a top-hatful of feathers into a leather casing, which was then rounded and hand-stitched. No two balls weighed the same, and their shape varied as well - and by quite a lot after a round of golf!

A major step forward was made in 1845 when Reverend Robert Paterson invented the "gutty," which was molded out of **gutta-percha**, a gum substance from Malaya. The first gutty was used at the Blackheath Club; and, because it was round and

thus gave the ball a true flight, it became very popular.

One problem with this new ball was that it fell from the sky like a dead bird without completing its true trajectory. However, this problem mysteriously cured itself toward the end of a round. It was realized that this was happening because of the damage done to the ball during the round. Golf balls began to be manufactured with the "damage" already done, leading to the "dimpled" golf ball of today.

The gutty was eventually phased out after the American Coburn Haskell developed the rubber-core ball in 1898. His ball failed to receive the immediate acclaim of the day's top professionals, but when Alex Herd won the 1902 British Open after outdriving his rivals, that all changed. There was a

Above Two "featheries" used in the 1840s.

Right This top hat full of feathers was required to make one "feathery" ball.

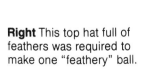

rush to acquire Haskell balls, which were made by wrapping an elastic thread around a rubber core with a gutta percha, later a balata cover. This was the three-piece ball; and manufacturers were, and still are, constantly experimenting with dimple design and arrangement in an effort to design a ball that will achieve ever-greater distance.

The three-piece ball has, however, made way for the two-piece in recent years, consisting of a solid rubber core and a durable cover, usually made of Surlyn℗. Yet another improvement to help the present-day golfer.

Top The evolution of the golf ball from the original wooden ball through to the rubber-core ball.

Above A golf ball press.

Above Willie Park, Sr., the first British Open champion.

Left What the late 19th century golfer looked like. Willie Park, Jr., with caddie John Carey.

PLAYING THE GAME

IT IS IMPORTANT that any budding golfer should realize from the outset that the likes of Nick Faldo, Jack Nicklaus, Arnold Palmer, Tom Watson, Seve Ballesteros, and Curtis Strange didn't suddenly become good golfers. They have spent many years developing their innate skills. True, the high handicap golfer will go out and hit the occasional wonderful drive straight down the middle of the fairway. And true, he will think "this is easy." But what happens next? He approaches his second shot with a 4-iron, slices it out of bounds, and it's back to the drawing board.

   To get from tee to green is *not* easy, and in this chapter we will attempt to familiarize you with the basic golf swing, highlight the common errors that creep in, and hopefully point you in the right direction to make that short journey from tee to green.

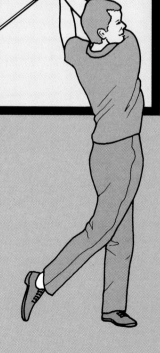

UNDERSTANDING THE GOLF CLUB

MANY PEOPLE, WHEN they decide to take up golf, go out and spend a lot of money on equipment without really understanding what they are buying.

Because golf equipment *is* expensive, it is important to know what to look for. If you look through any golf magazine, you will be lost in a maze of graphite shafts, persimmon heads, single-unit clubs, cavity-back irons, and so on. These are all modern technological improvements which are designed to make the game easier, and they do work. But the best tools in the hand of a poor craftsman don't guarantee good work. Likewise with golf clubs.

THE FIRST STEP: WHAT TO BUY

If you look at a full set of clubs laid out in a shop, you will instantly see that each is a different length. But don't forget, sets do come in different lengths. So, just because a set of clubs looks good and feels good on the grip, they may not be the right length for you. A further look at each club reveals that the lie (angle between shaft and head) varies; this lie alters the swing path. So, you must know which lie is ideal for your swing path. You must be sure to select clubs with the right lie for your height and physique.

So where do you go for the correct advice? Any PGA professional will be only too pleased to advise on the correct clubs for you, a service that many retail outlets often do not provide. But this advice is important. You are making a big investment when you buy a set of golf clubs, and you and your clubs have got to be compatible.

DO YOU NEED A FULL SET OF CLUBS?

The simple rule is "buy within your budget." But remember, the most clubs you are allowed to carry in your bag is 14. The top professionals carry the maximum, but they know exactly what they can achieve with each club. The club player with a full set will use only half of them on a regular basis, will occasionally give the others an airing, play a bad shot, and leave them in the bag for six months.

Ideally a half set, consisting of a 3-wood, 3-, 5-, 7- and 9-irons, a sand wedge, and a putter, is enough for the novice to get going. Of course, the more you play and the more you enjoy the game (and maybe get better at it as well) the more you will want to add to your set of clubs. But for the time being, settle for a half set.

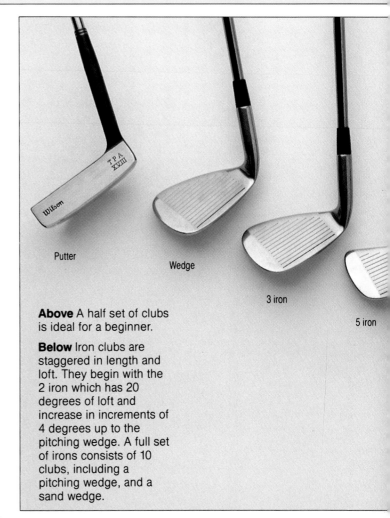

Putter   Wedge   3 iron   5 iron

Above A half set of clubs is ideal for a beginner.

Below Iron clubs are staggered in length and loft. They begin with the 2 iron which has 20 degrees of loft and increase in increments of 4 degrees up to the pitching wedge. A full set of irons consists of 10 clubs, including a pitching wedge, and a sand wedge.

7 iron

9 iron

3 wood

THE MODERN GOLF BALL

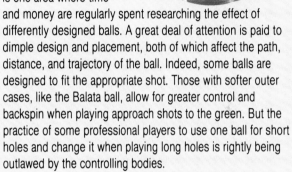

As manufacturers constantly attempt to keep up to date with modern technology, they are always seeking to make the game of golf easier for players at all levels, particularly professionals.

Golf ball manufacture is one area where time and money are regularly spent researching the effect of differently designed balls. A great deal of attention is paid to dimple design and placement, both of which affect the path, distance, and trajectory of the ball. Indeed, some balls are designed to fit the appropriate shot. Those with softer outer cases, like the Balata ball, allow for greater control and backspin when playing approach shots to the green. But the practice of some professional players to use one ball for short holes and change it when playing long holes is rightly being outlawed by the controlling bodies.

As modern balls are assembled in two pieces, attention is paid to the compression of the inner part of the ball without compressing it too much or too little. Balls with a greater compression ratio should, when hit correctly, travel farther than one will with a low ratio. But hit a high compression ball wrong, and boy, can it hurt!

But the key to all this rests on the ability and skill of the player with the club. A good-quality high compression ball in the hands of a player who hasn't a clue what to do with the club is a waste of time and money.

DID YOU KNOW?

A Japanese company is planning to introduce a new golfing product - the biodegradable tee. Usually made of wood or plastic, many tees are lost during the course of a game, littering golf courses. Apparently the Japanese version turns into compost within hours.

ANATOMY OF A GOLF CLUB

THE GOLF CLUB consists of a head, shaft, and handle. As mentioned earlier, modern designs provide a wide choice for all golfers, professional and amateur alike. But, no matter whether you select steel-shafted, graphite-shafted, wooden heads, or metal heads, the make-up of the golf club is the same.

The **handle** is the part of the club you hold and is known as the grip. Look at the grip; you will see a pattern on it. This pattern is not just to make it look pretty, but to help you make sure your club is aligned properly when addressing the ball. If the pattern is off-center, you have not addressed the ball in the correct manner.

The **club head** is made up of the face, the toe, the heel, and the most important part: the **leading edge**. The leading edge is the bottom edge of the club face, and this is the part of the club head that must be lined up with the ball and square to it and the target line at address. Many novices believe the top of the club should be used to square up against the ball at address. This is wrong. It is important *now* that you understand the leading edge, because it forms the basis of every golf shot. The leading edge is *always* at right angles to the ball and target line, no matter whether you are playing with an open or closed club face.

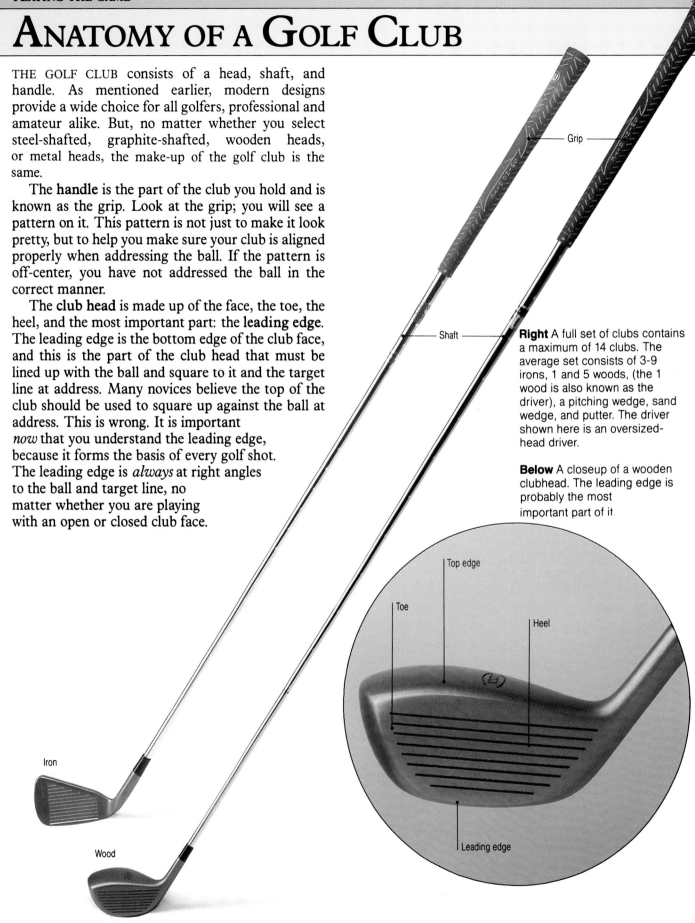

Grip

Shaft

Iron

Wood

Top edge

Toe

Heel

Leading edge

Right A full set of clubs contains a maximum of 14 clubs. The average set consists of 3-9 irons, 1 and 5 woods, (the 1 wood is also known as the driver), a pitching wedge, sand wedge, and putter. The driver shown here is an oversized-head driver.

Below A closeup of a wooden clubhead. The leading edge is probably the most important part of it.

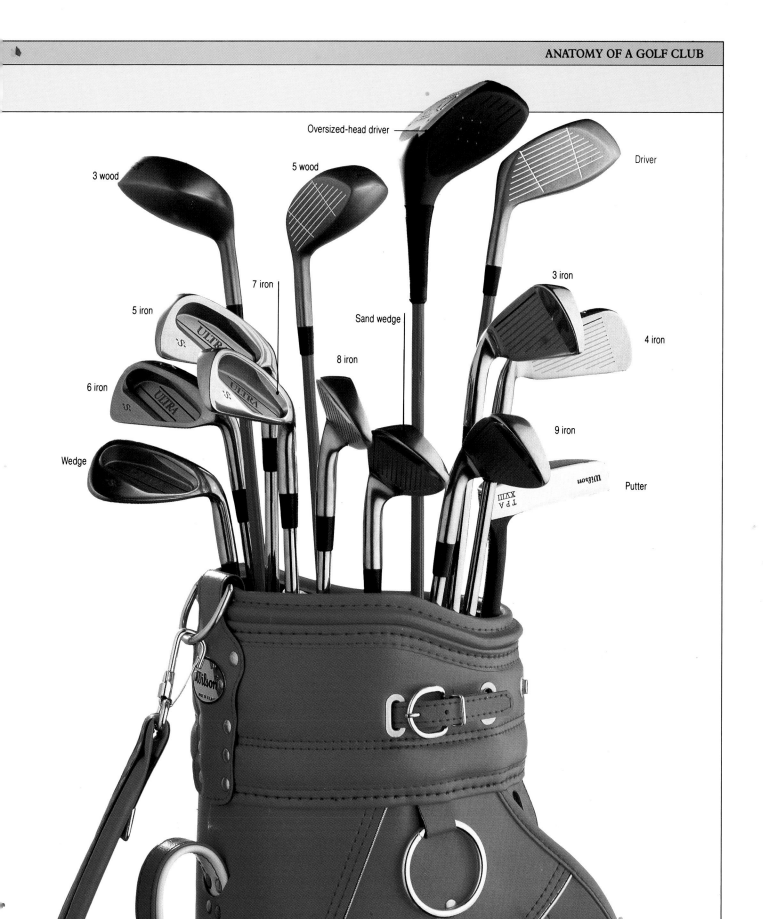

Oversized-head driver

Driver

3 wood

5 wood

7 iron

3 iron

5 iron

Sand wedge

4 iron

8 iron

6 iron

9 iron

Wedge

Putter

THE GRIP

THE FIRST STEP toward mastering the basic golf swing is to learn how to hold the club. The left hand (assuming you are a right-handed player) is the more important of the two hands in the grip. It is the dominant hand yet only the 3rd, 4th and 5th fingers actually grip the club.

To establish the correct grip, open your left hand and place the club handle diagonally across the palm. Close your hand, making sure the last three fingers grip only the handle. Your other finger, and thumb, merely play a "supporting" role - literally.

To check if you are holding the club correctly with your left hand, ground the club head in the address position, and keeping your left arm straight, you will see that a "v" has been formed by your thumb and index finger. If you are holding the club correctly, this "v" should be pointing to a spot between your head and right shoulder.

Now for the right hand. This time, only the second and third fingers apply pressure on the handle. The other fingers, and the thumb, are again to give support. But where exactly do you put all of your fingers? Well, there are three basic grips, and each is designed to suit personal needs, depending on the size of your hands. Try all three before you find the one you feel most comfortable with. However, none will feel particularly comfortable at first.

ESTABLISHING THE GRIP

To establish the correct grip, take the club in your left hand (below left), making sure it is comfortable. Close your hand (below right). Place the club handle in your right hand as shown (near right). The second and third fingers only of the right hand should apply pressure. Finally, adopt the address position (far right). Note that your right shoulder will dip slightly once this position has been established.

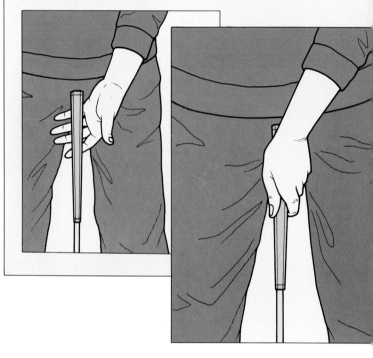

THE OVERLAPPING GRIP

More commonly known as the grip, as in *"The Vardon Grip"* after champion golfer Harry Vardon who made it popular at the turn of the century, this is the most popular of the three grips. Having applied pressure with the second and third fingers of your right hand, rest the little finger on top of the index finger of your left hand. Ground the club as before and this time you will see that both hands have created a "v" as previously mentioned. For the grip to be correct, *both* "v"s must be aiming toward that point between your head and right shoulder.

THE INTERLOCKING GRIP

Popular among golfers with smaller hands, this grip is similar to the overlapping grip, but this time the little finger of the right hand and index finger of the left are interlocked. Again, check that your "v"s are pointing the right way.

THE TWO-HANDED GRIP

This is sometimes called the "double-handed grip" because all fingers of both hands make contact with the club handle and with one hand above the other. This grip is the least popular and least used of the three, but is often used by people who are unable to place a strong grip on the handle.

The key thing to remember with this grip is those "v"s. Make sure they are always aiming at that point between your head and right shoulder. This applies no matter what club you are using. Wayward shots can be caused by many factors, but more often than not, they stem from the very beginning - the grip. So make sure it is right from the start.

This information will be the opposite way around if you are left-handed. However, for the remainder of this book, we will give instructions for right-handed players. Left-handers should do things in reverse.

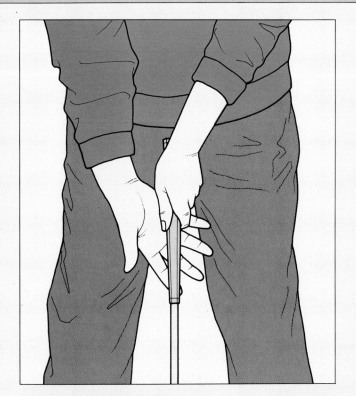

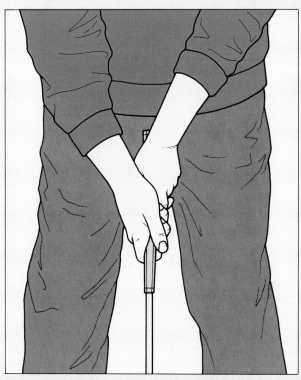

The two-handed grip.

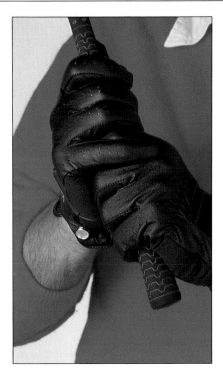

The overlapping grip, known as the Vardon Grip.

The interlocking grip with the index finger of the left hand and little finger of the right hand interlocking.

THE STANCE AND THE ADDRESS

THE CORRECT STANCE and address are vital to achieve your ball-to-target line via the correct swing path. The **ball-to-target line** is the direction in which you intend to send the ball toward a pre-determined target.

There are three types of **swing path:** *inside-to-square,* *out-to-in,* and *in-to-out.* But, to understand what that means, you must first understand what is meant by *outside* and *inside.*

When you take up your normal stance, your feet are *inside* the target line. The area on the other side of the target line is the *outside.*

The normal golf stroke follows a path whereby the clubhead is taken back on the *inside,* is brought down, makes contact with the ball, and follows through on the *inside.* This is known as the *inside-to-square* swing path. A clubhead taken back on the outside, but traveling inside on the follow-through is known as an *out-to-in* swing path; the *in-to-out* path is the opposite.

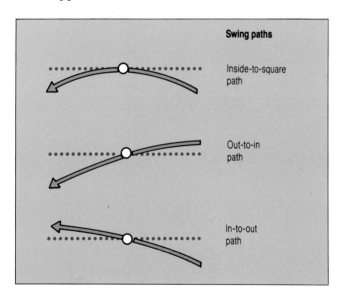

Swing paths

Inside-to-square path

Out-to-in path

In-to-out path

THE STANCE

You are probably familiar with the "keep the left arm straight" theory. Well, the left arm does have to be kept straight most of the time, but don't fall into the trap of believing the left arm and club must be kept straight and rigid as one unit. They don't.

To adopt the correct position of your left arm, hold it down by your side. Now clench your fist as if you were holding a club, and then insert a club into the clenched hand. You will see that an angle has been created between your left arm and the club.

This is the correct setting of the left arm and is how your left arm and club should look when the ball is being addressed. This is where novices fall down; they believe the left arm should be straight *and* the club should be an extension of that arm as one straight unit.

Bob Tway, the surprise winner of the 1986 US PGA Championship, defied all the rules of the basic swing. His stance was cumbersome, he had a hunched back, and he placed his hands low down the club handle. Yet he won a Major.

You are now holding the club correctly and have adopted the correct left arm position. Now it is time to address the ball.

THE ADDRESS

It is important to get your posture correct at address. Don't bend your knees too much: this is a common fault with high-handicap golfers. They tend to think that the knees are the most important part of the body in the address position. They are not. That privilege belongs to the spine. It is important that you obtain the correct spinal angle.

To obtain the correct spinal angle, stand upright and bend your back forward slightly so that your rear end is sticking out slightly. Now bend your

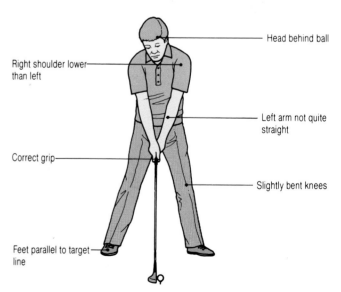

Head behind ball

Right shoulder lower than left

Left arm not quite straight

Correct grip

Slightly bent knees

Feet parallel to target line

Above Note how the head is behind the ball, the distance between the feet, and the position of the ball in relation to the left heel.

Right This picture shows that the left arm and club are not one straight unit.

knees, and you have adopted the correct posture. Try and imagine yourself sitting on the edge of a high stool - that is what the correct posture should be.

Your grip is now right, left arm is OK, and posture is fine. But that is not the end of it. We now have to make sure the shoulders are in the right position. The shoulders are an integral part of the golf swing. If they aren't working properly, the whole swing will fall apart. There is a lot to learn about this golf swing, but, if you get it right at the outset, you will always have a good swing.

The ideal shoulder position should be with your right shoulder slightly lower than your left. This is achieved by moving your head so that it is slightly behind the ball in the address position. If it is not behind the ball you will have an unbalanced swing, and this means problems.

Your head plays a crucial role in the golf swing. How often have you heard the expression "he lifted his head too quickly"? People don't say that for the sake of it. Poor use of the head *does* result in a poor golf shot.

The head should be kept in the same position - slightly behind the golf ball - throughout the swing and even at the moment the club and ball make contact. It should only be lifted on the follow-through after impact. But we will come to that later. So: *keep your head steady during the swing.*

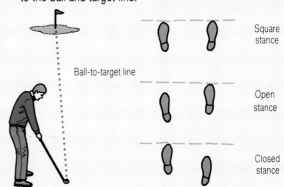

YOUR QUESTIONS ANSWERED

Q How do I establish the target line?

A Imagine a straight line drawn from the ball to the target. That is the target line. To make sure you are standing in the correct position at address, you must be standing parallel to the target line to establish what is called a **square stance**. Therefore, imagine another line drawn in front of your feet. This line should be parallel to the target line. If your left foot is drawn back from this line, you are said to have adopted an **open stance** and your entire body will be aiming to the left of the intended target. A **closed stance** is when the left foot is forward of the right and the body is pointing toward the right of the intended target.

Having adopted a correct square stance, line the club up with the ball, making sure the leading edge is square to the ball and target line.

Square stance

Ball-to-target line

Open stance

Closed stance

Q How far apart should my feet be when addressing the ball?

A There is no golden rule on this subject. The choice of club and your own physical make-up will dictate this to a large extent. But, as a general rule, the inside of your shoes should be even with your shoulders when playing with a wood; when you use a short iron, like a wedge, the outside of your shoes should be even with your shoulders. But the secret is to be comfortable.

Q How high should I tee the ball when driving?

A When you use a wood, the general rule is to make sure about half of the ball is showing above the top of the clubhead. But this is only a guideline. If you are playing into a strong headwind, you would tee the ball up lower than usual. The most important rule is *not to tee the ball too high.* When using irons, you don't need to tee the ball as high as when using a wood.

SWINGING THE CLUB

IF, AFTER DIGESTING the foregoing about hold, posture, head position and so on, you still want to play golf then read on. But be warned, there is still much more to learn about the golf swing!

There is only one golf swing - whether you are playing a full-blooded drive off the tee or a 9-iron approach shot to the green, the swing is the same, although modified to fit the shot.

The first action of the golf swing after address is the takeaway, and like all other aspects of the swing, it is crucial that you have a good takeaway. Get it wrong and the chance of the remainder of the swing being wrong is very high.

The takeaway is achieved by taking the clubhead backwards from the ball and at the same time rotating the entire left side of your body toward the right, which is possible because your right hip and shoulder move backwards slightly at the same time

as the takeaway. It is important to make sure that your elbows are kept the same distance apart during the takeaway as they were at address.

THE BACKSWING

The takeaway is the first part of the backswing, which follows in one continuous and fluent movement as you take the club above your head.

A successful backswing is achieved by cocking the wrists correctly at the right time. The wrists should cock naturally during the backswing, and the shorter the club, the earlier they cock. With a driver, they do not cock until they are nearly at the top of the backswing.

We have already mentioned keeping the left arm straight; it should be kept straight at all times,

THE BLUEPRINT GOLF SWING

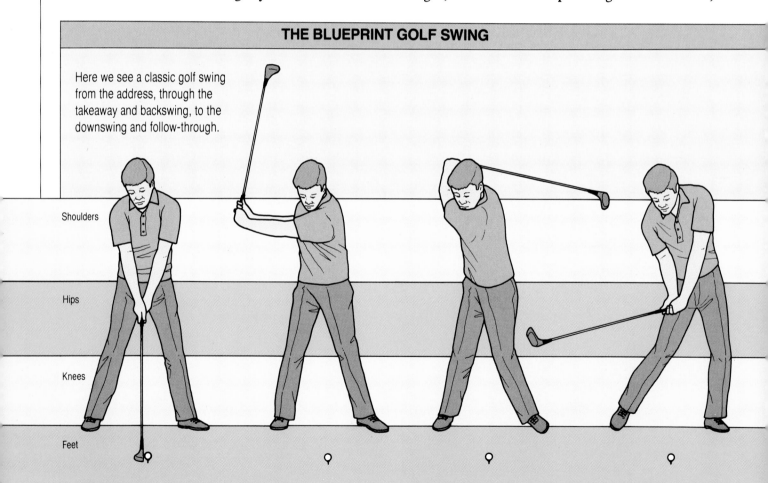

Here we see a classic golf swing from the address, through the takeaway and backswing, to the downswing and follow-through.

Shoulders

Hips

Knees

Feet

Comfortable address - not too tense.

Straight left arm on takeaway

Head behind the ball and kept still. Right elbow pointing at the ground behind the right heel.

Weight transferred to the left leg immediately before contact.

although it is not necessary for it to be rigid. At the top of the backswing, it is virtually impossible to keep it rigidly straight even if you try. Keep it as straight as you can, but feel comfortable.

At the top of the backswing, your right elbow should be pointing toward the ground slightly behind your right heel, and the club shaft should be pointing toward the target and parallel to the ball-to-target line. Your elbows should have kept the same distance apart throughout the backswing.

There is no need to rush the takeaway and backswing. Take a look at Larry Nelson. His takeaway is very deliberate, as is his backswing, and they result in a lovely, rhythmic swing. Top US money winner Corey Pavin also has a fluent swing, and on the European Tour Sam Torrance boasts one of the best swings, thanks to his slow deliberate action. Ian Woosnam also has a fluent swing. He makes it look so easy, but he, a smaller than average man, can pack awesome power into those clubs.

Once the clubhead has reached the top of the backswing, it has to start the downswing, its return journey to the ball, which, like all other aspects of the swing, is very important, because everything must come down as it went up for the clubhead to make the correct contact with the ball.

THE DOWNSWING

The hips play a key role in the downswing; they move slightly ahead of your hands so that the weight can be transferred from your right side to your left leg, which will enable you to keep your body square with the ball at impact. It is important that you keep your head still during the downswing and that you

Head remains still and everything is back to where it started at address.

The follow through starts.

The club is raised, and the head automatically starts to lift as the eyes begin to follow the ball.

The end of the swing. The clubhead is behind the head and the toes of the right foot pointing toward the ground.

Shoulders

Hips

Knees

Feet

maintain the correct spinal angle.

You may think that is the end of the swing. But it is not. The swing doesn't end at the moment the clubhead makes contact with the ball. There is also the very important follow-through.

THE FOLLOW-THROUGH

After making contact with the ball, allow the clubhead to continue on its natural journey until it swings behind your head. As you follow-through, the action will automatically lift your head, so there is no need to lift it early to see where your ball has gone. Many novices make the mistake of lifting their head as soon as they make contact with the ball. A good follow-through will bring your head up automatically and at the right time. If you have followed through correctly, your balance will be transferred entirely to your left leg, and your right knee will be facing the target with the balance of your right leg transferred to your right toe.

Two final tips on the swing.
• Always keep your eye on the ball, but remember: when playing your shot, you should concentrate on looking at the back of the ball.
• Maintain good balance through the entire swing. To test your balance, try to hold your follow-through position until the ball has landed. If you can manage this, give yourself a pat on the back: you have maintained perfect balance.

Johnny Miller executes an impressive follow-through at the 1991 Open at Birkdale.

YOUR QUESTIONS ANSWERED

Q How do I cure slicing and hooking?

A Slicing off the tee is probably the most common fault that novices encounter. When you look at the list of possible causes it is hardly surprising. The most common fault is striking the ball with an open club face. In other words, the leading edge is not at right angles to the ball and target line. Instead, it is pointing to the right of the target. This is often caused by a poor takeaway or, more likely, a weak grip with one or both hands too far around the club handle.

An incorrect address position, normally by having the ball too far forward in relation to your feet, will lead to the slice. This is because the shoulders are open, and not square at address. An open stance is also a likely cause of the slice.

Again, there are many possible causes of the hook. This time, a strong grip, with one or both hands too far to the right around the handle, will be a likely cause. Closec shoulders at address will probably cause a hook, which will stem from having the ball positioned too far back at address.

Having the left elbow too close to the body in the back- and downswing are other common causes, as is over-swinging at the top of the backswing, when the club goes too far at the top of the swing and is pointing to the right of the intended target. But the most common cause of the hook is closing the clubface at impact. Check to see where your hands are at address. If they are too far forward, it is a simple matter to rectify.

Q What is a push shot? Is it like a slice?

A No, it isn't like a slice. A slice is when the ball starts by aiming toward the intended target but then veers right. The push is when the ball travels to the right of the intended target but in a straight line. This is more often than not caused by incorrect alignment with the target line at address.

Q Is the pull therefore the opposite of the push?

A Yes, except this time the ball is "pulled" to the left of the target instead of the right with the push. Like the push, it is often a well-struck shot, but alignment at address was wrong.

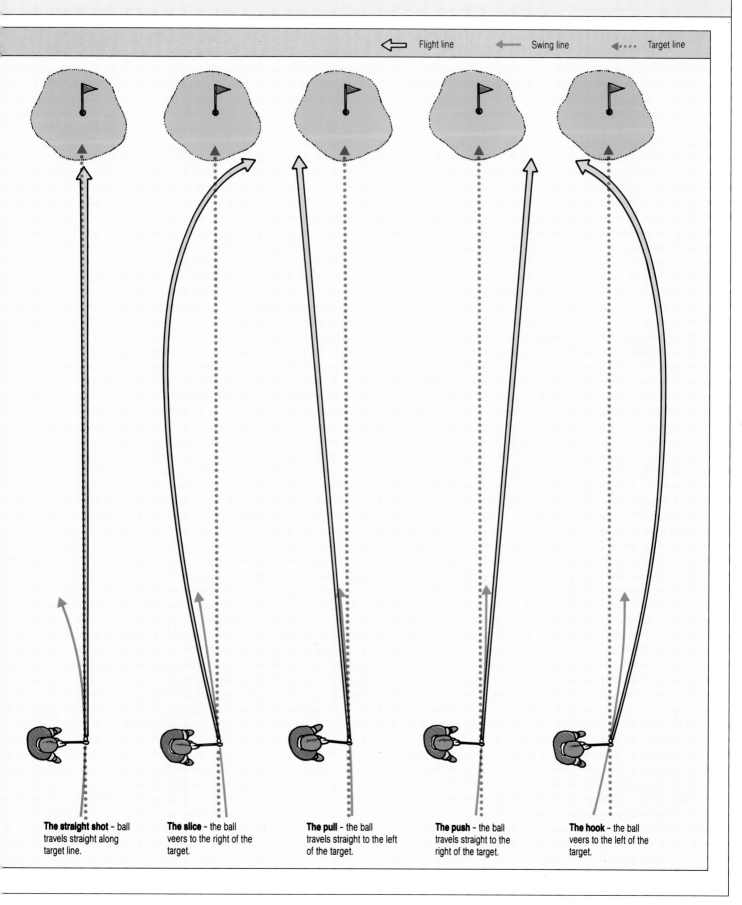

Flight line   Swing line   Target line

The straight shot – ball travels straight along target line.

The slice – the ball veers to the right of the target.

The pull – the ball travels straight to the left of the target.

The push – the ball travels straight to the right of the target.

The hook – the ball veers to the left of the target.

ONTO THE FAIRWAY

PROVIDED YOU HAVE mastered the basic swing, all other golf shots should now become a mere formality. But there are certain pointers that you should bear in mind when adapting the basic swing to specific shots.

PLAYING FAIRWAY WOODS

Many high-handicap golfers find the use of the fairway wood for extra distance an awesome prospect. But, if you have the blueprint swing correct, it need not be; if played correctly, you will gain some extra valuable yards on each round. Don't, however, think that you have to use a wood every time you are on the fairway. You have to analyze your next shot and decide whether a wood will be more beneficial than an iron. Only you can make that decision, and only when you are faced with your next shot.

The position of your ball on the fairway will dictate whether you take a wood or iron. If you have a poor lie, leave the wood in your bag. However, if your ball is lying in a good position, take the wood out if you feel it will benefit you. But don't think you are the next Nick Faldo or Jack Nicklaus by taking out your No. 1 wood. Try a more lofted club like a 2-, 3-, 4-, or 5-wood. The best tip when deciding whether to play the wood is make sure the leading edge sits nicely on the ground. If it does, you should be fine with that club. If not, seriously consider changing it. It is also advisable to close your stance slightly, but only slightly, when playing fairway woods. This will help you to get your right shoulder out of the way during the backswing.

PLAYING LONG IRONS

The long irons are those between a 1- and 4-iron. Again, a slightly closed stance should be adopted so that you can get your right shoulder out of the way in the backswing. Other than that, play the shot normally; because you are playing a long iron, you need to play the shot with a full swing. Remember, the longer the iron, the nearer to your left heel the ball should be at address. As you use the 4-iron, the position of the ball should be moving nearer to a position halfway between your two feet. But, if you have adopted the correct hold and posture, this should now become second nature.

One of the best long-iron players is Britain's Sandy Lyle. He generates a great deal of power, but a close look at his swing reveals a gentle and smooth takeaway, the start of any successful swing.

PLAYING THE MEDIUM IRONS

The medium irons are regarded as the 5-, 6-, and 7-irons. By now, the ball position at address should have moved toward the center of your feet with it moving slightly nearer to your right foot with the 7-iron. But, don't forget, you must also make sure your head is still behind the ball. The temptation is now to move it over the ball. Resist it!

You will have noticed that the clubs are now getting shorter. Consequently, when you adopt your stance, you will find yourself standing closer to the ball. Furthermore, the gap between your feet will

PLAYING WITH FAIRWAY WOODS

Playing with a fairway wood is little different from playing a wood off the tee. The position of the ball in relation to the left heel should be the same, and the width of shoulders should be equivalent to the width between the insides of your feet.

Stance and posture remain the same when playing fairway woods. A slightly, but only *slightly*, closed stance will help the swing.

have closed and your shoulders should now be, approximately, even with the outside of your shoes.

There is no need to adopt a slightly closed stance when playing medium irons; you should adopt a square stance, and because the clubs are now shorter, your stance will be more upright, which should result in a shorter swing.

PLAYING WITH SHORT IRONS

The other irons, 8- and 9-iron, and the two wedges are regarded as the short irons. The feet are moved closer together when playing with these irons, the ball is in a position closer to the right heel, and a slightly open stance is adopted. When taking a very short swing you need to get your body out of the way quickly after making contact with the ball, and a slightly open stance helps you to do so.

PLAYING WITH SHORT IRONS

When playing irons, the shorter the iron, the closer the feet are positioned together. The outside of the shoes should be even with your shoulders.

The shorter the iron, the nearer you should stand to the ball at address. But length of club dictates this distance. Open your stance slightly when playing with shorter irons. It will help to get the left side of your body out of the way quicker in the backswing.

YOUR QUESTIONS ANSWERED

Q I find that I often top the ball when playing a fairway wood or with a 1- or 2-iron. Why is this?

A First of all, it is important to realize that you don't have to lift the ball into the air – the club is designed to do that for you. That already gets rid of one of the causes of topping, trying to lift the ball off the ground.

Having the ball too far forward or standing too far away from the ball at address are two major causes of topping. Poor weight distribution during the back- and downswing will result in your head coming up too soon. The result is topping.

Playing with a tense grip is often a cause of topping, but many players don't realize they are holding too tightly. The whole body then becomes tense, which results in an upward movement of the body at the moment of contact. If you do realize you are feeling tense at address, walk away from your address position and start over again. It is remarkable how much difference it will make to your play if you are relaxed at address.

Another simple cause of topping is taking the wrong club to a ball in relation to its lie.

Q And what about fluffing?

A Fluffing is another of those embarrassing shots that creeps into the novice's game. It is when the clubhead strikes the ground at the back of the ball before making contact with it. The most common cause is having the ball positioned too far back at address. To compensate, the back- and downswing then have to be altered, resulting in a last-minute stabbing at the ball, with disastrous consequences.

Q Why am I now taking divots with medium and short irons?

A Because your swing is now more upright, and the angle at which the clubhead approaches the ball creates a divot. Don't worry, there is nothing wrong with taking a divot, but *you must always*, REPEAT, *always, replace any divots* you take. Golf courses take plenty of hammering as it is. Try and spare them by replacing your own divots and any others left by inconsiderate golfers.

PITCHING AND CHIPPING

FIRST OF ALL, it is important to appreciate the difference between pitching and chipping. The **pitch** is played by using a lofted club (9-iron or wedge, or similar) on to the green. Depending upon conditions and amount of backspin applied to the ball, it will either stop dead on landing, roll or spin forward slightly, or even roll or spin backwards. The **chip**, however, is played with a less lofted club and is played onto the green, but then runs on toward the target.

The decision whether to pitch or chip rests solely with you. But, don't forget, course conditions must be taken into account. A rock-hard putting surface is not the best to pitch to because the ball will probably run on after pitching. In this case a delicate chip and run will be the best shot. A damp fairway and green will lend itself better to the pitch as will a ball sitting up nicely in lush grass. And don't forget, if it is a windy day, a pitched ball will be affected.

The pitch is played mainly with the arms and hands; the full golf swing is not necessary. But all the other rules of the swing apply. Play a "miniature" swing, not a full-blooded one; that is not necessary because the pitch is made only when the ball has a very short distance to travel.

Make sure the leading edge is square to the ball and ball-to-target line, and open your stance slightly, because you have to transfer your weight from your right leg to your left quicker than normal because of the shortness of the backswing. But remember, there will be very little transfer of weight when playing a pitch or chip. When playing short pitches onto the green, shorten your club slightly by moving your hands down the handle.

When playing a lofted shot, the ball will make a pitch mark on the green. Before you make your putt,

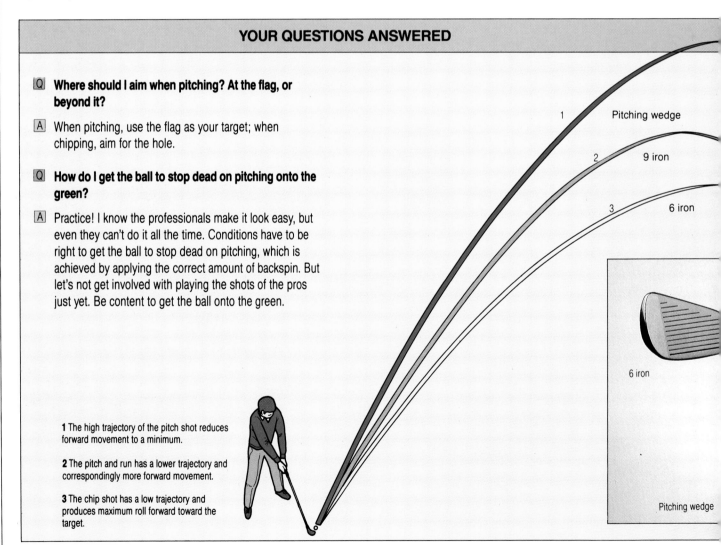

YOUR QUESTIONS ANSWERED

[Q] **Where should I aim when pitching? At the flag, or beyond it?**

[A] When pitching, use the flag as your target; when chipping, aim for the hole.

[Q] **How do I get the ball to stop dead on pitching onto the green?**

[A] Practice! I know the professionals make it look easy, but even they can't do it all the time. Conditions have to be right to get the ball to stop dead on pitching, which is achieved by applying the correct amount of backspin. But let's not get involved with playing the shots of the pros just yet. Be content to get the ball onto the green.

1 Pitching wedge

2 9 iron

3 6 iron

6 iron

Pitching wedge

1 The high trajectory of the pitch shot reduces forward movement to a minimum.

2 The pitch and run has a lower trajectory and correspondingly more forward movement.

3 The chip shot has a low trajectory and produces maximum roll forward toward the target.

repair it. This is part of the etiquette of the game.

The **chip** is usually played with a less lofted club, not one of the short irons. This time, the intention is to loft the ball not high into the air, but only slightly, and then to get it to run on toward its target after landing.

Again you should adopt an open stance and shift more of your weight onto your left leg. Shorten the club by moving your hands down the handle and take some of the loft off the club by moving your hands forward a little bit.

Two of the finest exponents of chipping and pitching in the modern game are the Spaniards José-Maria Olazabal and Seve Ballesteros. Olazabal is a master at pitching while Ballesteros is a master at chipping. Watch how Seve makes full use of his knees when chipping, as does the top American golfer, Tom Watson.

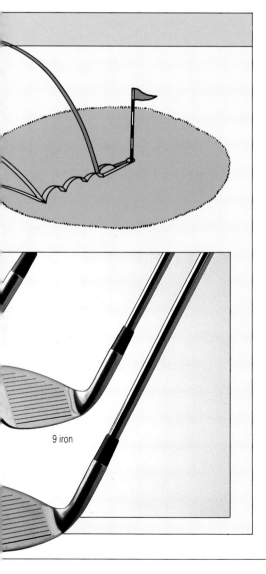

9 iron

Above right The study of concentration . . . Severiano Ballesteros following his ball out of a bunker.

GETTING OUT OF BUNKERS

WATCH THE LIKES of Gary Player, Paul Azinger, Scott Simpson, and "Big Momma" JoAnne Carner, and getting out of bunkers seems like just another easy aspect of the game. But, in reality, the traps are so strategically placed that they should in some way handicap those wayward shots and certainly for the high-handicap player they do just that. But, once the fear of the bunker shot is overcome, landing in the sand should not prove too costly.

Player, Azinger, Simpson, and Carner are all excellent sand players because they have one thing in common: they have spent hours practicing the bunker shot, realizing how important it is to get out of the bunker cleanly and accurately. So, the first hint is *practice*. It is, perhaps, the one aspect of the game that the club player neglects. But it is just as important as driving, pitching, and putting.

There are two types of bunker: the **fairway bunker** and the **greenside bunker**. Let us look at the fairway bunker first.

The one thing you must remember when playing from a **fairway bunker** is not to be too ambitious.

PLAYING OUT OF A GREENSIDE BUNKER

When playing out of greenside bunkers, adopt a very open stance (A). Keep your eye fixed on the sand just behind the ball (B). Make contact with the point behind the ball on which you have fixed your eyes (C). A correct contact will see the sand lift the ball out of the bunker (D).

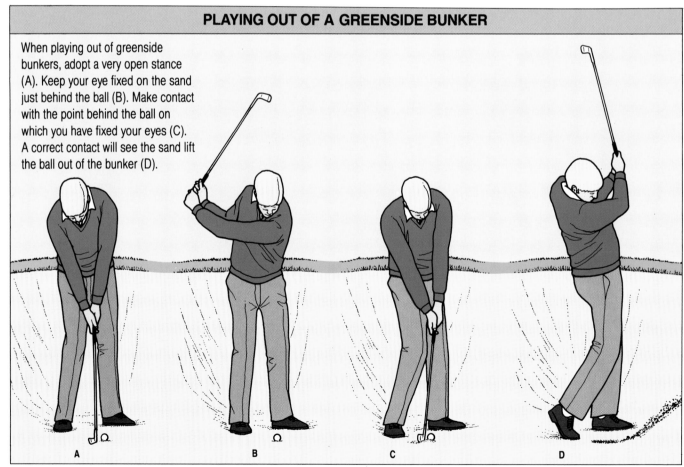

A   B   C   D

Left Gary Player learned at an early stage in his career that it was crucial to be able to play good and accurate bunker shots, and he spent hour after hour playing out of traps.

Right Britain's Laura Davies playing out of a bunker during the 1991 Women's Open.

OK, Fred Couples played a wonderful shot from a fairway bunker on his way to winning the 1992 US Masters. But he's Fred Couples. Your ball may be sitting up nicely, and you think, "I can hit the green with a 4-iron." What happens next? Your confidence gets the better of you, the ball is not hit properly, it catches the lip of the bunker, and back into the sand it rolls.

It is recommended that you take something between a 5- or 7-iron, or even a utility wood, like a 5- or 7-wood. Make sure your stance is square, not an open one as when playing out of greenside bunkers. Focus your eyes on the back of the ball as normal, but make sure you don't take sand first. Take the ball first.

Your ball may be lodged in the bunker so that it is impossible to come out forward. In that case, don't try to be ambitious. If you have to play out sideways or backwards, then do so. It may well be your best option. One thing to remember about bunker play is that you must *not* ground your club in the sand, and the first time the clubhead makes contact with the sand is when you play the shot. If you do ground it earlier, you will be penalized two strokes in medal play and forfeit the hole in match play.

The approach to **greenside bunkers** is very different because you have very little room to work in, and you must get the ball out cleanly, but then get it to stop on the green.

Before you enter the bunker, weigh up your shot and get an idea of the distance you have to play. In the bunker, get your feet comfortable and open your stance. Make sure the ball is lined up with your left heel. It is important this time when opening your stance that your shoulders should follow the same line as your stance and not remain square to the target line. For this shot, the leading edge of the club should, however, be square to the ball and the target line.

The backswing is mostly a wrist and arm action and is made along the line of your shoulders, not the target line. Concentrate your gaze on the area of sand approximately 2in. (5cm) behind the ball because it is here that the clubhead is going to strike.

The clubhead is not going to strike the ball. Because the club face is open, and you apply an "out-to-in" swing, it will travel under the ball and lift it out of the sand.

Before finishing with bunkers, there are two important etiquette rules that you should remember.
• Always enter the bunker from the back, not the front.
• After playing your shot, rake over all your footprints.

DID YOU KNOW?

The word "caddie" comes from the French word "cadet." The first player to use a caddie or "cadet" is believed to be the Marquis of Montrose in the early 17th century.

PUTTING

HAVING DONE THE seemingly hard part and hit that little white ball the quarter of a mile from tee to green, it now comes down to the "simple" task of putting the ball into that hole. But how often is a potentially good score ruined by poor putting?

This part of the game must be practiced more than any other because, don't forget, a saved shot on every putting green reduces your round by 18 strokes. That can make the difference between a round of 100 and one of 82. Doesn't 82 sound a lot better than 100?

When putting, everything you have learned about the basic golf swing must be forgotten because we are going to start afresh.

First, adopt a different grip. The most popular is the reverse overlap, but it is one of those areas where you have to find a grip that you feel comfortable and successful with. First try the reverse overlap, and then modify it if you want to.

To achieve the reverse overlap, nine of your ten fingers (the index finger of your left hand being the exception) grip the club handle. All four fingers and the thumb of the right hand grip the handle with the thumb resting on the flat part (if there is one). The last three fingers and the thumb of the left hand also grip the handle, again with the thumb resting on the flattened part. The other finger, the index finger, rests across the fingers of the right hand.

The putting stroke is not played with the wrists. They should remain uncocked as the stroke is made with the arms, shoulders, and club acting as a single unit and moving accordingly.

Your head should now be positioned directly over the ball, not behind it as it is during the basic golf shot. But your head must remain still throughout the putting stroke.

The club face should be lined up square with the ball and target, with the ball lined up with the middle of the putter. There is usually a marker on top of the putter head to indicate the middle of the club face.

Positioning the ball at address in relation to your feet is a personal thing. Most players line it up with their left toe, but when you look at the top professionals, you will see a wide variety of putting actions. But all are effective, some more than others. Payne Stewart, for example, has a very upright putting stance with the toe of the putter on the ground and the heel off it. But he still sinks those putts!

A good weight distribution, evenly between both

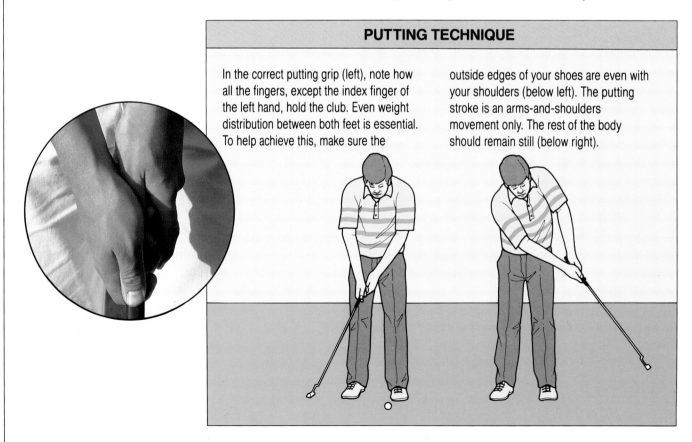

PUTTING TECHNIQUE

In the correct putting grip (left), note how all the fingers, except the index finger of the left hand, hold the club. Even weight distribution between both feet is essential. To help achieve this, make sure the outside edges of your shoes are even with your shoulders (below left). The putting stroke is an arms-and-shoulders movement only. The rest of the body should remain still (below right).

YOUR QUESTIONS ANSWERED

Q What is meant by "reading" the greens?

A Not all putting surfaces are perfectly flat and level, in fact very few are. All have some undulations or individual peculiarity which must be identified before making a putt. There may be a roll from the left to the right, it may be an uphill putt, a downhill putt, and so on. You must walk around the green to establish this before attempting your putt. But once you have decided which way the green rolls, or whatever, you must make allowance for it with your putting stroke by aiming more to the left or right, or hitting it with more or less power. But you must remember that *all putts are straight*. It is the borrow of the green and speed the ball is hit which determine in which direction it travels. One word of advice about putting: make your mind up about the putt and *don't change it*.

Q What are the important things to remember when first putting out?

A To begin with, the person farthest from the hole always plays first. If the ball is on the putting surface, the flag must be either out of the hole or tended, but it must be taken out as soon as the ball is played. Any person holding the flag must remain perfectly still during the putting stroke, and all other playing members should remain still, quiet, and keep out of the line of sight while another player is putting.
Second, if your ball is just off the green, you can opt to have the flag out, left in, or tended. If you opt for it to be left in and the ball strikes it before entering the hole, there is no penalty.
Finally, a round of golf can take a long time to complete, and there is nothing worse than having to wait while a match takes time to clear the green ahead, because they are marking their cards, or analyzing putts. Get the putting over with quickly and leave the green for the next match. When you approach the putting area, note where the next hole is so that you can place your bags, ready to move on.

feet, is essential for good putting, and to help achieve this it is ideal to have your legs apart so that the outside of your shoes are even with your shoulders.

It cannot be stressed too much that you should spend time on the practice greens. That is what they are there for. And when putting, don't be too ambitious. If you can get down in two putts on every hole, you are well on your way to becoming a low handicap player. Don't attack the hole with every shot. Imagine the hole as being six feet wide. If it were, you would hole every putt in one. So, aim to get the ball into that six-foot hole, and if you manage that each time, then you are left with an easier second putt. But it is those putts from about six feet that you should be practicing.

The putting surfaces are carefully manicured and are the pride and joy of every groundsman. His skill in preparing the green must never be forgotten or abused. Therefore, there are some very important points to remember on the putting surface.

Do not take pull carts onto the green and don't put your golf bag on the putting surface. Make sure your, and other unrepaired, pitch marks are repaired, and when you take the flag stick out of the hole, don't throw it onto the green; place it gently.

Bob Charles was one of the game's finest putters and was the most outstanding left-handed golfer. He captured the British Open title in 1963.

AWKWARD SHOTS

UPHILL AND DOWNHILL lies often trip the novice up, but they are not as difficult as they seem, provided the necessary adjustments to the basic golf swing are made.

THE UPHILL LIE

When faced with an uphill lie, the first thing you must do is set the body so that it is perpendicular to the ground. The ball should be farther back in the address position than you would normally expect with the same club. Because the ball will be "taking off" on the up slope, you will also need to make allowances when choosing your club by selecting a less lofted club.

A slight in-to-out swing path should be adopted. This will result in the ball's being hooked slightly, so aim marginally to the right of your intended target. Keep your head still throughout the shot.

THE DOWNHILL LIE

The downhill lie is much more difficult to play than the uphill lie. Again, your body must be perpendicular to the ground. But, because you are leaning to the left, you must control your head and make sure it is still positioned behind the ball. It is not easy, but it is essential to the shot.

The ball should again be slightly back in the address position, and because of the position of the ball, a more lofted club should be selected. This time, an out-to-in swing path will probably be created, so you therefore need to aim slightly to the left of the target to compensate for the slice.

PLAYING THE BALL BELOW YOUR FEET

Balance is the key word again. The tendency this time is to lean forward with your weight distribution moved to your toes. To compensate, bend your knees more than usual to maintain a good balance. Hold the club near the end of the handle and position the ball halfway between your two feet at address. Aim marginally to the left of your target because the downswing will naturally create a shift of balance to your toes and an out-to-in swing path will result, thus creating a slice.

Top Playing the uphill lie. Note how important it is to keep the body perpendicular to the ground.

Above For a downhill lie, the body should be kept perpendicular to the ground.

Above When playing the ball below your feet, bend your knees more than normal and aim slightly to the left of your target to compensate for the slice.

Above right Adopt a more upright stance when playing with the ball above your feet and aim to the right of your target.

PLAYING THE BALL ABOVE YOUR FEET

This time you have to shorten the club by holding it farther down the handle. The ball should still, however, be positioned halfway between your two feet; but, because the flat swing created by your stance will create an in-to-out swing path, you must aim to the right of your intended target to compensate for the hook.

BALL AT THE FRONT OF A BUNKER

You must first realistically assess your chances of getting out of the bunker. Remember what we said about being overambitious. If there seems to be no way out at the front of the bunker, look at the options of playing out sideways or backwards.

However, if you do have a shot, you have to approach it in a different manner than you would use in playing a conventional shot from the bunker. Because of the ball's position, you will be standing in a very difficult position, with one leg higher than the other, so it is important to maintain good balance. Placing a lot of weight on your left leg will help with your balance. You should make sure your stance is very open. After that, play your normal bunker shot.

BALL AT THE BACK OF A BUNKER

A ball positioned close to the back of the bunker generally poses more problems because you may have to play the shot standing outside the bunker. Whether you are standing in or out of the bunker, you must create a very upright backswing to prevent

catching the edge of the bunker with the clubhead. The upright swing will open the club face at impact, and it is important that you follow the swing through correctly.

BALL PLUGGED IN A BUNKER

Adopt a square stance, not an open one, and have the ball positioned halfway between your two feet. Make sure the clubhead is closed and blast the ball out of the sand. The soft sand will cause the closed face to open on impact. Make sure you follow through after impact - if you can!

PLAYING OUT OF THE ROUGH

The rough is that uncut area on each side of the fairway. The rough on the fringe of the fairway is often not as severe as that beyond it and is known as the light rough. Quite often it is easy to play out of the light rough, and it may make little or no difference to the outcome of your score on the hole. If the ball is "sitting up," there is no reason why you shouldn't use a wood out of the light rough.

If it is "sitting up," it is resting on top of the rough, which is longer than the fairway grass. Therefore, when you adopt your stance, your feet will be firmly on the ground, and your ball will be higher than normal. To compensate for this and to prevent your clubhead from passing directly underneath the ball, you should shorten the club by moving your hands down the handle.

The long grass, or deep rough, poses more problems, and it is here that we again use that word "ambition." Perhaps you would be better taking a 9-iron and pitching back onto the fairway? Don't forget, if you are in big trouble in the deep rough, it is because you played a bad shot in the first place.

Left Bunkers like this are a daunting prospect for the club player, but to Australia's Greg Norman, one of the Winged Foot "monsters" poses no problem.

Below right Severiano Ballesteros is the master of the recovery shot, and it is no problem for him to recover from long rough like this.

What makes you think that you are now capable of following it with a superhuman shot as a means of recovery? Come on! Leave that to the likes of Seve

Again, your lie will dictate which club you choose, but you are recommended to use a club with a heavier head, like a 9-iron or wedge. Otherwise, the clubhead will be likely to get entangled in the long grass, and a heavier clubhead will help overcome this to a certain extent. Remember that a utility wood, 5- or 7-wood, will be heavy enough in many cases to get your ball out of the deep rough without getting the shaft tangled in the grass or undergrowth.

It is important that you attack the ball with an upright backswing which will again help prevent the club from getting entangled in the grass. However, if you are in the deep rough, you may be surrounded by trees, bushes, and so on, and they will all dictate what kind of backswing you can use.

You can only learn a certain amount about this wonderful, if at times frustrating, game from a book. The rest is up to you. Mental attitude, and the time and desire to practice, will make you a better player. And expert guidance and advice is strongly recommended. You are well advised to have a few lessons with a PGA professional before you pick up too many bad habits.

DID YOU KNOW?

Some long-standing golf superstitions maintain that it is bad luck to enter the clubhouse and find a black cat sleeping on your golf bag; to stumble on the steps leading from the fourth tee; to have a robin alight on the iron marker of the hole you're approaching; to leave your pencil in the locker and have to borrow one from your opponent.

GOLF GREATS

THE WORLD OF golf has provided many great personalities. They have spanned many eras, starting from the early days of championship golf back in 1860. GREAT PLAYERS is a selection of some of those whose names will always be part of golfing lore.

A Tour is a season-long series of events which finds the best golfers, whether they be male or female, junior or senior players, competing against each other for much sought-after prize money. GREAT TOURS takes us around the world with some of the most exciting players whoever walked the course.

All the world's leading golfers compete against each other regularly, but during the year they gather for events like the British and US Opens, Masters, PGA Championship, and so on. The GREAT TOURNAMENTS gives an insight into these exciting, top-class events.

GREAT PLAYERS: MEN

SEVERIANO BALLESTEROS
(Spain, born 1957)
Ballesteros first attracted attention when he finished joint second in the 1976 British Open at the age of 19. He then went on to win the Open in 1979 and the following year became the youngest winner of the US Masters. He has won more than 50 events on the European Tour and his worldwide career earnings are in excess of £3 million.
Majors (5): *British Open 1979, 1984, 1988; US Masters 1980, 1983*

JAMES BRAID
(Great Britain, born 1870, died 1950)
Along with Harry Vardon and J. H. Taylor, James Braid was one of the Great Triumvirate who dominated British golf at the turn of the century, when they won the British Open 16 times between them. In later life Braid was a highly respected golf course designer.
Majors (5): *British Open 1901, 1905-06, 1908, 1910*

Right James Braid.

Below The "Great Triumvirate" of J. H. Taylor (standing right), James Braid (seated left), and Harry Vardon (seated right) are joined by another turn-of-the-century great, Sandy Herd.

Seve Ballesteros

BILLY CASPER
(United States, born 1931)
Billy Casper's record of 51 US Tour wins puts him sixth on the all-time list, with only the game's greatest names in front of him. A member of eight Ryder Cup teams, he has three Majors to his credit, and after joining the US Seniors Tour in 1981, he continued adding to his tally of successes.
Majors (3): *US Open 1959, 1966; US Masters 1970*

HENRY COTTON
(Great Britain, born 1907, died 1987)
Britain's finest golfer in the 1930s and 40s, Henry Cotton is the only man to win the British Open both before and after World War II. He won his first Open at Sandwich in 1934 with a round of 65, which was to remain unbeaten until 1977.
Majors (3): *British Open 1934, 1937, 1948*

Nick Faldo

Henry Cotton

NICK FALDO
(Great Britain, born 1957)
In recent years the British have dominated world golf, none more so than Nick Faldo, who has taken on the Americans and beaten them on home soil. He has won the British Open three times, and in 1990 became only the second man after Jack Nicklaus to retain the US Masters title. His career earnings have reached the $5 million mark.
Majors (5): *British Open 1987, 1990, 1992; US Masters 1989-90*

WALTER HAGEN
(United States, born 1892, died 1969)
The flamboyant Walter Hagen deserves a lot of credit for the recognition that professional golfers of today now receive. He

Walter Hagen

BOBBY JONES
(United States, born 1902, died 1971)
Bobby Jones was the world's greatest amateur player, and such was his record that he was a match for any of the day's professionals, including Walter Hagen. In 1930 Jones achieved the greatest grand slam in golf when he won the amateur and Open titles of *both* the United States and Great Britain.
Majors (7): *British Open 1926-27, 1930; US Open 1923, 1926, 1929-30*

TOM KITE
(United States, born 1949)
The biggest money winner in US golf history, Tom Kite looked like being stuck with the tag "the best man never to win a major," until 1992 when he captured the US Open. Two years earlier, he became the first man to win more than $6 million on the US tour.

Tom Kite

identified himself with the ordinary man and exploded the myth that golf was played by a select few. He was a great character; furthermore, he was a great golfer and was one of the finest match play exponents in the 1920s.
Majors (11): *British Open 1922, 1924, 1928-29; US Open 1914, 1919; US PGA 1921, 1924-27*

BEN HOGAN
(United States, born 1912)
The golf world was dominated by three men from the late 1930s to

40s: Sam Snead, Byron Nelson, and Ben Hogan. Hogan's stylish play kept him at the top for more than a decade. Best remembered for his courageous comeback following a road accident in 1949, he went on to win the US Open the following year after being told he would never walk again. In 1953 he won three Majors, something no other man has done in a single year.
Majors (9): *British Open 1953; US Open 1948, 1950-51, 1953; US Masters 1951, 1953; US PGA 1946, 1948*

Texas-born Kite was runner-up to Larry Wadkins in the 1970 US Amateur Championship and turned professional two years later.
Majors (1): *US Open 1992*

BOBBY LOCKE
(South Africa, born 1917, died 1987)
South Africa's first great golfer was Bobby Locke who, along with Australia's Peter Thomson, dominated the British Open in the 1950s. Famous for his knickers and white cap, Locke won more than 80 tournaments worldwide, including several on the US circuit in the early post-war years.
Majors (4): *British Open 1949-50, 1952, 1957*

Bobby Locke

TOM MORRIS, JR.
(Great Britain, born 1851, died 1875)
Young Tom Morris is probably the finest golfer that ever lived. A professional at the age of 14, he won his first British Open at only 17, and by the age of 20 he had won four titles. He is the only man to win four successive titles (there was no competition in 1871). He would doubtless have won more had he not died at the age of 24 following a bout of depression after his wife and newborn baby had died in childbirth.
Majors (4): *British Open 1868-70, 1872*

TOM MORRIS, SR.
(Great Britain, born 1821, died 1908)
The first of the greats of Championship golf, Old Tom Morris, like his son, won four British Open titles. He was also a

Two of golf's greatest players; Old Tom Morris (left) and his son.

great match player and along with another great of the game, Allan Robertson, formed an invincible team. Morris started his career as an apprentice ballmaker with Robertson.

Majors (4): *British Open 1861-62, 1864, 1867*

BYRON NELSON
(United States, born 1912)
Nelson holds a place in golfing history because, in 1945, he won a US Tour record of 18 events in one season, including a staggering 11 consecutively. At the peak of his career, he went 113 tournaments without missing the cut, and his total of 52 US Tour wins puts him fifth on the all-time list.

Majors (5): *US Open 1939; US Masters 1937, 1942; US PGA 1940, 1945*

JACK NICKLAUS
(United States, born 1940)
Jack Nicklaus is unquestionably the finest golfer of the modern era, and his record of 18 professional Majors is seven more than the next best man, Walter Hagen. Nicklaus achieved his victories at a time

Jack Nicklaus

Byron Nelson

when the golf world was littered with many talented players, thus making his achievement even more outstanding. The US Amateur champion in 1959 and 1961, he made a name for himself in the 1960 US Open when he pushed Arnold Palmer all the way before losing by two strokes. The "Master" of Augusta, Nicklaus has won the title a record six times, including 1986 when he was 46. Since joining the Seniors Tour, he has continued his winning ways.

Majors (18): *British Open 1966, 1970, 1978; US Open 1962, 1967, 1972, 1980; US Masters 1963, 1965-66, 1972, 1975, 1986; US PGA 1963, 1971, 1973, 1975, 1980*

GREG NORMAN
(Australia, born 1955)
Greg Norman burst onto the international scene in 1980 when he captured the French Open,

Australian Open, Scandinavian Open, and World Matchplay championship at Wentworth. He has since won many other tournaments in his homeland, Europe, and the United States, where he has twice been the top money-winner. However, he still has just one Major to his credit, even though he came close to capturing all four in 1986. He led all four championships going into the final round, only to see three titles taken away from him. The only one he captured was the British Open.

Major (1): *British Open 1986*

FRANCIS OUIMET
(United States, born 1893, died 1967)
The amateur changed the whole face of world golf when he took on and beat two of Britain's best

Francis Ouimet (center) with Harry Vardon (left) and Ted Ray (right), 1913

Arnold Palmer

professionals, Harry Vardon and Ted Ray, by five and six strokes, to win the play-off and take the US Open at Brookline, Massachusetts, in 1913. His victory opened the door for American golf, and his countrymen never looked back. Ouimet won the US Amateur title twice, in 1914 and 1931.

Major (1): *US Open 1913*

ARNOLD PALMER
(United States, born 1929)
Arnold Palmer is the man who popularized golf in the 1960s. Furthermore, he was responsible for making sure that the British Open maintained its standing as the world's foremost tournament, because he convinced his fellow Americans to make the trip across the Atlantic each year. Palmer, along with his business partner, Mark McCormack, also improved standards and earnings for the professional golfer. He is owed a

huge debt by his fellow professionals and the golf world in general. On top of all that, Arnold Palmer was a very good golfer and remains one of the world's best-loved players.

Majors (7): *British Open 1961-62: US Open 1960; US Masters 1958, 1960, 1962, 1964*

GARY PLAYER
(South Africa, born 1935)
Along with Arnold Palmer and Jack Nicklaus, South Africa's Gary Player helped popularize golf in the 1960s, and for more than 30 years he has been delighting golf fans the world over. He alone has won the British Open in three different post-war decades, and his 22 wins on US soil is a record for a non-American.

Majors (9): *British Open 1959, 1968, 1974; US Open 1965; US Masters 1961, 1974, 1978; US PGA 1962, 1972*

Allan Robertson

Gary Player

ALLAN ROBERTSON
(Great Britain, born 1815, died 1859)
The name of Allan Robertson may not be a familiar one, but he was probably the first real great of golf in the pre-tournament days. Upon his death a tournament, the British Open, was inaugurated to find his "successor." As a match player, Robertson was unbeatable, and it is said that he never lost a head to head match.

GENE SARAZEN
(United States, born 1902)
Eugene Sarazen may have won seven Majors during his career, but he will always be remembered for two of golf's most memorable shots. The first was in 1935 on his

Sam Snead

although he was four times runner-up. When he won the 1965 Greater Greensboro Open, he became, at 52, the oldest winner on the US Tour. And in 1979 he shot his own age in the Quad Cities Tournament.
Majors (7): *British Open 1946; US Masters 1949, 1952, 1954; US PGA 1942, 1949, 1951*

JOHN HENRY "J. H." TAYLOR
(Great Britain, born 1871, died 1963)
Another of the Great Triumvirate along with Harry Vardon and James Braid, J. H. won five British Open titles. He turned professional at the age of 19 and later in life was largely responsible for the formation of the PGA as he sought to improve the professional's lot.
Majors (5): *British Open 1894-95, 1900, 1909, 1913*

PETER THOMSON
(Australia, born 1929)
Australian golf is enjoying a tremendous upsurge in the 1990s, but the man who started it all was Peter Thomson in the 1950s. He won a modern record-equaling five British Opens, including three in succession, and in seven consecutive years, 1952-58, he never finished lower than second. He was made an honorary member of the R & A in 1982.
Majors (5): *British Open 1954-56, 1958, 1965*

LEE TREVINO
(United States, born 1939)
Every sport needs its characters, and there is none greater in the world of golf than Lee Trevino. He makes the game fun; he also makes it look easy, and his record of 27 US Tour wins and career winnings in excess of $3 million confirm him as one of the all-time

greats of the game. In 1971 he achieved a remarkable hat-trick by winning the US, Canadian, and British Open titles within three weeks of each other.
Majors (6): *British Open 1971-72; US Open 1968, 1971; US PGA 1974, 1984*

HARRY VARDON
(Great Britain, born 1870, died 1937)
Jersey-born Harry Vardon was the most successful of golf's Great Triumvirate, winning the British Open a record six times. And his victory in 1914 completed the run of 16 Open wins in 20 years by Braid, Taylor and Vardon. He also won the US Open in 1900, and his victory helped spark off a great

Lee Trevino

way to winning his only Masters title when he holed a 220-yard four-wood shot at the par-5 15th for a double eagle. Thirty-eight years later at Troon, Sarazen holed the Postage Stamp (8th) in one during the British Open. His achievement was caught on camera to add to the glamour of the occasion.
Majors (7): *US Open 1922, 1932; British Open 1932; US Masters 1935; US PGA 1922-23, 1933*

SAM SNEAD
(United States, born 1912)
Sam Snead has won more US Tour events than any other man. His total of 81 is 11 more than second-placed Jack Nicklaus, but unlike Nicklaus, Snead never captured the top prize in US golf, the Open,

Peter Thomson

deal of interest in the game in America.

Majors (7): *British Open 1896, 1898-99, 1903, 1911, 1914; US Open 1900*

TOM WATSON
(United States, born 1949)
With 32 US Tour wins, over $5 million career winnings, and five British Opens to his credit, Tom Watson is rightly on the list of all-time best golfers. His British Open record is a remarkable modern-day achievement, and he is still playing well enough to equal Harry Vardon's record one day.

Majors (8): *British Open 1975, 1977, 1980, 1982-83; US Open 1982; US Masters 1977, 1981*

Tom Watson

GREAT PLAYERS: WOMEN

PATTY BERG
(United States, born 1918)
A teenage prodigy, Patty Berg gained recognition by reaching the final of the US Amateur as a 17-year-old. She turned professional in 1940. Off the golf course, as the first president of the US LPGA, she became acknowledged as one of the game's outstanding female figures.
Major victories: *US Amateur 1938; US Open 1946; World Champion 1953-55, 1957*

JOANNE CARNER (née GUNDERSON)
(United States, born 1939)
Known as "Big Momma," JoAnne

JoAnne Carner

Carner has been thrilling US crowds for more than 30 years. In 1987, at the age of 48, she came close to winning the US Open, but lost a three-way play-off (won by Britain's Laura Davies). JoAnne Gunderson won her first of five Amateur titles at the age of 18. She did not turn professional until she was 30.
Major victories: *US Amateur 1957, 1960, 1962, 1966, 1968; US Open 1971, 1976*

SANDRA HAYNIE
(United States, born 1943)
Birdies at the last two holes enabled Sandra Haynie to capture her first US Open in 1974 by one stroke. She has won four women's Majors, capturing the LPGA title twice, the Open once, and the Du Maurier Classic once. She joined the US Tour in 1961 and was the top Tour winner in 1974 and 1975 with 10 victories.
Major victories: *US Open 1974; US LPGA 1965, 1974; Du Maurier Classic 1982*

BETTY JAMESON
(United States, born 1919)
After a successful amateur career that yielded two Amateur titles, Betty Jameson became one of the pioneers of the women's professional game in the post-war years. She was runner-up in the first US Open in 1946 and came back to win the following year by six strokes. She retired in 1965.
Major victories: *US Open 1947; US Amateur 1939-40*

CATHERINE LACOSTE
(France, born 1945)
One of France's leading lady golfers, Catherine Lacoste became the first amateur, and first non-American, to win the US Women's Open when she won at Hot

Sandra Haynie

Springs, Virginia, in 1967. She also became the youngest-ever winner. Two years later, she completed a notable double by winning the amateur titles of America and Britain in the same year. Catherine Lacoste is from a sporting family. Her father was tennis player René Lacoste, one of the famous French *Four Musketeers,* and her mother, Thion de la Chaume, won the British Open Ladies' Golf title in 1927. Catherine Lacoste was a member of France's World Amateur championship-winning team in 1964.
Major victories: *US Open 1967; US Amateur 1969; British Amateur 1969*

CECILIA LEITCH
(Great Britain, born 1891, died 1977)

Known as Cecil, she won a record four British Amateur titles between 1914 and 1926. She had made her debut in the championship in 1908, her first serious competition, and she introduced power and mastery of woods not previously seen in the women's game. In addition to winning titles in Britain, Cecilia Leitch captured five French Open titles and in 1921 had a remarkable 17 and 15 win to take the Canadian Open.

Major victories: *British Amateur 1914, 1920-21, 1926; English Ladies 1914, 1919*

NANCY LOPEZ
(United States, born 1957)

Nancy Lopez made an immediate impact in her debut season as a professional by finishing second in the US Open. She has gone on to confirm that early promise and become one of the biggest money winners on the US Tour with over $3 million. After winning her 35th Tour event in 1987, she was inducted into the Hall of Fame.

Major victories: *US LPGA 1978, 1985, 1989*

CAROL MANN
(United States, born 1941)

In winning the 1965 US Open, 6ft. 3in. tall Carol Mann showed great determination to come back after shooting an opening-round 78 and

Left Nancy Lopez

Below Carol Mann

Above Joyce Wethered

Left Louise Suggs

make up a seven-stroke deficit. A member of the ladies tour since 1961, she was top money-winner in 1969 and has enjoyed nearly 40 Tour wins, including eight in her top money-making season.
Major victory: *US Open 1965*

BETSY RAWLS
(United States, born 1928)
One of the early greats of the ladies professional tour, Betsy Rawls won the first of four US Opens in her debut season as a professional in 1951. The previous year she was runner-up as an amateur. The leading money winner in 1952 and 1959, she

ended her career with 55 Tour wins. She later became president and then tournament director of the LPGA.
Major victories: *US Open 1951, 1953, 1957, 1960; US LPGA 1959, 1969*

LOUISE SUGGS
(United States, born 1923)
After a very successful amateur career which saw her win the US and British amateur titles in successive years, Louise Suggs turned professional and vindicated her decision by winning all the major honors the game could offer. In addition to winning the US

Open twice, she was runner-up no less than five times. Her efforts for improving the lady professionals' standing was rewarded with her appointment as president of the LPGA in 1956. She won 50 Tour events.
Major victories: *US Open 1949, 1952; US LPGA 1957; US Amateur 1947; British Amateur 1948*

GLENNA VARE (née COLLETT)
(United States, born 1903)
A great favorite with spectators and fellow professionals, Glenna Collett's record of six US Amateur titles, including three in

succession, is likely to remain unbeaten for a long time. She was captain of the US Curtis Cup team four times.
Major victories: *US Amateur 1922, 1925, 1928-30, 1935*

JOYCE WETHERED

(Great Britain, born 1901)
Joyce Wethered, a student of Harry Vardon and J. H. Taylor in her early days, won five consecutive English

Kathy Whitworth

championships and four of the six British championships she entered. The great Bobby Jones once described her swing as "one of the best ever" by man or woman. Indeed a great compliment for one of Britain's best-ever lady golfers.
Major victories: *British Open 1922, 1924-25, 1929; English Championship 1920-24*

KATHY WHITWORTH

(United States, born 1939)
The most successful golfer on the US Women's Tour with 88 wins. Like her male counterpart, Sam Snead, she too has never won the US Open, although she has captured six women's Majors. Kathy Whitworth carried on where Mickey Wright left off and became the sport's premier lady throughout the 60s and 70s.
Major victories: *US LPGA 1967, 1971, 1975*

MICKEY WRIGHT

(United States, born 1935)
Mickey Wright's 82 Tour wins are second only to Kathy Whitworth's all-time record of 88. She was invincible in the 1960s and was top money winner four years in succession from 1961 to 1964, during which time she won 44 tournaments, including a record 13 in 1963. She had great power, and her presence considerably improved the standard of the women's game. Her total of 12 Majors is a women's record.
Major victories: *US Open 1958-59, 1961, 1964; US PGA 1958, 1960-61, 1963*

MILDRED "BABE" ZAHARIAS (née DIDRIKSON)

(United States, born 1915, died 1956)
Didrikson acquired the name "Babe" after her baseball idol

Babe Zaharias

Babe Ruth. An all-round sportswoman, she won two track and field gold medals at the 1932 Olympics before turning to golf. She became equally successful at her new sport, and after winning the 1946 US Amateur title she became the first American to win the British title a year later. She then turned professional and in 1948 won the US Open. She was top money winner in the LPGA Tour's first four years, when she registered 19 of her 31 Tour wins. She lost her fight against cancer in 1956.
Major victories: *US Open 1948, 1950, 1954; US Amateur 1946; British Amateur 1947*

US PGA TOUR

THE US TOUR effectively started with the launch of the US Open in 1895; and four years later, when the Western Open was first played, it became a "two-event tour." But the forerunner of the modern-day Tour started in the 1920s, when club professionals from all over the United States met in the winter months to play a series of competitions in the warmer southern states, starting on the West Coast and moving around to the East Coast by spring before eventually returning to their club jobs for the summer months.

With the likes of Walter Hagen, Bobby Jones, and Gene Sarazen joining the Tour, it became very popular, and by the end of the decade the Los Angeles Open, Pensacola Open, Texas Open, and Western Open were all annual fixtures. The Western Open, dating to 1899, is the oldest event on the US calendar after the US Open.

Other tournaments became regular fixtures in the 1930s. There were the Bing Crosby Pro-Am, Phoenix Open Invitational, Greater New Orleans Open Invitational, and Greater Greensboro Open.

Despite a financial decline in the United States, the golf Tour still continued to attract large galleries during the 1930s as it continued to grow in popularity with both players and spectators alike. And it was during this period that some of the next generation of leading American golfers were spawned, including Sam Snead, Byron Nelson, and Ben Hogan.

After World War II the Tour became more structured and organized. Prize money increased, and the Tour developed rapidly when television became a regular "spectator." Sponsors lined up to

be associated with individual events, and this revenue, together with television rights, meant that winnings soared.

The touring professionals took control of the events in 1968 when they formed the Tournament Players Division.

Prize money on offer today exceeds $50 million per season. But the money doesn't all go to the professionals. The PGA Tour is proud of its slogan which says: "The leading money winner on the US PGA TOUR is Charity," because, since 1984, it has donated more than $100 million to various charities.

Action from the 1988 Players Championship, won by Mark McCumber. The Championship is played at the US PGA Tour's headquarters at Sawgrass, Ponte Vedra, Florida.

Such is the demand to join the Tour that a satellite tour was established, and players finishing outside the top 125 on the money list each season have to compete along with other aspirants, in an end-of-season "school," to regain or gain their card to play on the Tour.

US PGA TOUR RECORDS AND MILESTONES

Records

Most tournament wins:	81 Sam Snead (1936-65)
Most wins in one year:	18 Byron Nelson (1945)
Most consecutive wins:	11 Byron Nelson (March-August 1945)
Most money won in a career:	$6,655,474 Tom Kite (1972-91)
Lowest 72-hole score:	257 Mike Souchak (1955 Texas Open)
Lowest 18-hole score:	59 Al Geiberger (1977 Memphis Classic)
	59 Chip Beck (1991 Las Vegas Invitational)
Oldest winner:	52 yrs. 10 mths. Sam Snead (1965 Greensboro Open)
Youngest winner:	19 yrs. 10 mths. Johnny McDermott (1911 US Open)
Most times top money winner:	8 Jack Nicklaus (1964-65, 1967, 1971-73, 1975-76)

Milestones
Career

First player to win $1 million:	Arnold Palmer (July 21, 1968)
First player to win $2 million:	Jack Nicklaus (Dec. 1, 1973)
First player to win $3 million:	Jack Nicklaus (May 22, 1977)
First player to win $4 million:	Jack Nicklaus (Feb. 6, 1983)
First player to win $5 million:	Jack Nicklaus (Aug. 20, 1988)
First player to win $6 million:	Tom Kite (Aug. 5, 1990)

Season

First player to win $100,000:	Arnold Palmer (1963)
First player to win $250,000:	Jack Nicklaus (1972)
First player to win $500,000:	Tom Watson (1980)
First player to win $750,000:	Curtis Strange (1987)
First player to win $1 million:	Curtis Strange (1988)

DID YOU KNOW?

On February 6, 1971, astronaut Alan B. Shepherd, Jr., hit a golf ball 200 yards on the moon, making golf the first sport to be played in outer space and maybe paving the way for a future intergalactic tour!

Above Deane R Beman, the US PGA Tour Commissioner was a first class golfer and twice won the US amateur title before turning professional.

Left A great golf fan and supporter of the US Tour, comedian Bob Hope.

THE EUROPEAN PGA TOUR

THE EUROPEAN PGA Tour, now known as the Volvo Tour because of its sponsorship package with the Swedish car manufacturer, is the European equivalent of the US Tour, and each week 128 top professionals make their way across Europe in search of the £16 million prize money on offer during an eight-month season.

Like their American counterparts, British and European players have been competing together regularly in a series of events across Europe for many years, although most events were based in the British Isles.

The Tour as such really got underway in 1971, when John Jacobs was appointed by the PGA to make tournament play more financially viable and to organize it on a business level. In his first year, prize money was £250,000. Within four years he had doubled it. It was at that time that the Tournament Players separated themselves from the PGA, and in 1977 they merged with the Continental Tournament Players' Association to form the European Players' Division.

Prize money was then up to around £700,000, and the interest shown by BBC Television, and the

Right The Wentworth clubhouse. The Surrey course has been the home of the World Matchplay Championship since its launch in 1964.

Below Action from the Volvo Tour.

Tour's decision to switch events to a Sunday finish to fit into television schedules, proved to be canny, and in 1978 total prize money exceeded £1 million. Today, it is up to £16 million, and the number of tournaments has more than doubled from 17 in 1975.

On May 25, 1987, the Tour signed a deal with Volvo, which became their first corporate sponsor, and from that date the Tour became known as the Volvo Tour.

Like the American Tour, the European PGA Tour has its own Qualifying School each fall for all those players finishing outside the top 128 in the annual money list.

Nick Faldo, one of the top money winners on the European Tour, is seen teeing off at the 12th during the 1990 Volvo PGA Championship. However, it wasn't Faldo's year: victory went to Australia's Mike Harwood.

EUROPEAN PGA TOUR RECORDS AND MILESTONES

Records

Most tournament wins:	49 Severiano Ballesteros (1976-91)
Most wins in one year:	7 Norman von Nida (1947)
	7 Flory van Donck (1953)
Most consecutive wins:	4 Alf Padgham (1935-36)
	4 Severiano Ballesteros (1986)
Most money won in a career:	£2,691,090 Severiano Ballesteros
Lowest 72-hole score:	258 David Llewellyn (1988 AGF Biarritz Open)
	258 Ian Woosnam (1990 Torres Monte Carlo Open)
Lowest 18-hole score:	60 Baldovino Dassu (1971 Swiss Open)
	60 David Llewellyn (1988 AGF Biarritz Open)
	60 Ian Woosnam (1990 Torres Monte Carlo Open)
Oldest winner:	58 yrs. Alex Herd (1926 *News of the World* Matchplay)
Youngest winner:	19 yrs. 4 mths. Severiano Ballesteros (1976 Dutch Open)
Most times top money winner:	6 Severiano Ballesteros (1976-78, 1986, 1988, 1991)
Most money won in season:	£737,977 Ian Woosnam (1990)

Milestones

Season

First player to win £25,000:	Christy O'Connor (1970)
First player to win £50,000:	Severiano Ballesteros (1978)
First player to win £100,000:	Nick Faldo (1983)
First player to win £250,000:	Severiano Ballesteros (1986)
First player to win £500,000:	Severiano Ballesteros (1988)

OTHER TOURS

THE SAFARI TOUR is organized by the European PGA Tour and is held in the months leading up to the start of the Volvo Tour. Players make their way to the Central and Western African nations to compete in a mini 5-event tour that normally takes in Zimbabwe, Zambia, Kenya, Nigeria, and the Ivory Coast. It is popular with many of the European Tour players who are keen to prepare themselves for the forthcoming season in Europe.

The Safari Tour was launched in the mid-1970s, and the oldest of the five Opens is the Kenyan Open, which was launched in 1967. Sandy Lyle won his first major event when he captured the 1978 Nigerian Open, and his total of 124 for the first 36 holes is the lowest by any British professional. In the Pro-Am preceding the same event in 1973, David Jagger shot a world record-equaling 59.

The Asian Tour has gained in popularity in recent years as the Far East has become one of the biggest growth areas for golf, particularly in Japan. Consequently, large sums of money are being invested, and leading professionals are lured to the country each year. The growth of the sport in Japan is highlighted by the fact that Tommy Nakajima, the Ozaki brothers, and the lady golfer Ayoka Okamoto have all become world-class competitors in recent years.

The Asian Tour started life as the Far East Tour in 1959 when Eric Cremin, an Australian professional, and Kim Hall, a Welshman, organized the Hong Kong Open. The Tour was truly established on this foundation in 1961 when the Philippine and Singapore Opens were added to make it a three-tournament Tour.

Top One of Japan's leading players, Tsuneyuki "Tommy" Nakajima (left). Another Japanese golfer, Ayoka Okamoto (right).

Above The Ozaki Brothers, Joe (left) and "Jumbo" (right).

However, following the formation of the Asian Golf Confederation in 1963, the Tour blossomed; but it has only been in the last decade, since the leading American and European golfers showed interest in the Tour, that it has snowballed and is one of the wealthiest Tours outside the U.S.

Following the phenomenal growth of the sport in the country, the Japanese Tour was born separately out of the Asian Tour, and the large purses attract many top golfers to Japan each year.

The **Australasian Tour** has been responsible for providing such wonderfully talented players as Ian Baker-Finch, Rodger Davis, Greg Norman, Craig Parry, Mike Harwood, and others in the 1980s as Australia has emerged as one of the world's leading nations.

Because it is held during the US and European Tours' winter months, it gives the professional golfer the opportunity to play all year round. The three major events of the Tour are the New Zealand Open and the Australian Open and Masters.

South Africa has always produced fine golfers. First there was Bobby Locke and then Gary Player, and in recent years there has been a spate of other talented golfers, all of whom used the **Sunshine Tour** as their training ground.

Like the Australasian Tour, it is held during the US and European Tours' winter months, thus offering more competitive play to the world's top players in the southern hemisphere. The highlight of the South African season is the million-dollar challenge at Sun City every December, when invited players compete for the sport's richest prize.

Above The beautiful setting at Sun City, South Africa.

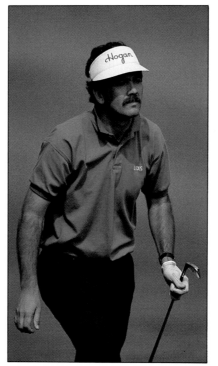

Above One of the current South African stars, David Frost.

Right Zimbabwe's Mark McNulty.

Right Now playing on the US Seniors Tour, Arnold Palmer remains as popular as ever and still attracts his "army" of fans.

Facing page (top) Marie-Laure de Lorenzi of France in action during the Weetabix British Open.

Facing page (below) Pat Bradley, the first woman to win more than $4 million on the US Women's Tour.

Back in the United States, there is the very popular **PGA Seniors Tour** which is open to players upon reaching their 50th birthday; and with Arnold Palmer, Jack Nicklaus, Gary Player, and Lee Trevino all beyond their 50th birthdays, the interest in the Tour is greater than ever as nostalgic memories are revived. The likes of Trevino and Nicklaus are winning more today on this Tour than they used to on the regular Tour. And in 1991 the top money winner on the Seniors Tour, Mike Hill, won over $1 million, more than Corey Pavin, the top money winner on the regular Tour.

The women have their own tours, and in the United States such is the popularity of the ladies' game that the **LPGA Tour** offers prize money that, in some tournaments, outstrips that offered in some men's events.

The LPGA (formerly the Women's Professional Golf Association, WPGA) was formed in 1944, but it struggled in its first couple of years. It was only after assistance from the Wilson sports goods company, and Fred Corcoran in particular, that the organization was marketed in the right way and the fortunes of the Association took an upward turn.

By 1952 the number of tournaments was up to 21 (from seven two years earlier), and "Babe" Zaharias, Betsy Rawls, and Louise Suggs became household names. The arrival of Mickey Wright attracted a great deal of media attention in the 1960s, and the women's game in the US again boomed. And in 1963 the Tour benefited from the arrival of the television cameras.

However, the Tour expanded too quickly and struggled to keep up with its expansion. In 1973 it had to be rescued from the verge of bankruptcy. The first commissioner, Ray Volpe, was appointed in 1975, and he set about seeking corporate sponsors. He succeeded and, in his seven years as commissioner, prize money soared from $1.5 to $6.4 million. Television coverage increased, as did the number of touring professionals, and the ladies' game in the U.S. went into the 1980s looking and feeling healthy.

Total purses from the 40-event schedule are in excess of $20 million, and the top money winner banks a check approaching the $1 million mark. Pat Bradley, the highest-earning lady player, has amassed career winnings of $4,109,165, only $1 million behind Jack Nicklaus.

The WPG European Tour however, does not enjoy the financial benefits of its American counterpart. It does not have the same sponsorship or television involvement as the US Tour, and consequently prize money and popularity are considerably lower. In 1992, the tour program had to be cut from 13 to 11 events because of sponsors' withdrawals. This compares to the 34 events on the US Women's tour in 1992.

THE BRITISH OPEN

Top The Red Moroccan leather championship belt that became the permanent property of Tom Morris, Jr., after his third British Open win in 1870.

Above Young Tom proudly wearing the belt.

THE WORLD'S FIRST Major, the British Open, inaugurated in 1860, was organized by the Prestwick club who sought to find a successor to Allan Robertson, the "champion of golf," who died in 1859. The only way to do that was by organizing an individual tournament, almost unheard of in those days. Most matches were foursomes or individual money matches.

But, in 1858, the Prestwick club had successfully organized an individual tournament for amateur players, and, following the suggestion of Major J. O. Fairlie, a similar tournament for professionals was arranged. On Wednesday, October 17, 1860, eight of Britain's leading professionals played three rounds of Prestwick's 12-hole links.

The winner was Willie Park, Sr., of the Musselburgh club. He was two strokes clear of local Prestwick man Tom Morris, Sr., who was to become one of the Open's great champions. Morris won the Open four times and was succeeded by his son, Young Tom, who also won the title on four occasions. Young Tom's untimely death at the age of 24 not only prevented him from adding to that total, but it robbed the game of one of its finest players.

The Open did not become "open" in the true sense of the word until 1861 when, again, organization was left to the Prestwick club. Old Tom Morris captured the title, and he, like all early winners, was presented with a Moroccan leather belt donated by the Earl of Eglinton.

The rules stipulated that the winner of the Belt three years in succession could keep the trophy, and so after Young Tom Morris won for the third time in 1870 he

THE FIRST OPEN IN 1860

On Wednesday, October 17, 1860, eight of Britain's top professionals met to play three rounds of Prestwick's 12-hole course.

Played in unsettled weather and in very windy conditions, Old Tom Morris of the host club was the first to tee off. Morris and Willie Park were the two favorites, and after the first round, Park led by three strokes, with a 55 to Morris's 58. The two men shot 59s in the second round as the Musselburgh man maintained his three-stroke advantage.

Morris was dogged by bad luck all day, and he could only make up one stroke on the leader in the final round, as Willie Park became the first Open champion with a score of 174.

Two days later, Morris beat Park by 7 & 6 in a £20 challenge match over the same 36 holes and thus regained some of his pride, and cash.

Scores
174 Willie Park, Sr. (Musselburgh)
176 Tom Morris, Sr. (Prestwick)
180 Andrew Strath (St. Andrews)
191 Robert Andrew (Perth)
192 George Brown (Blackheath)
195 Charlie Hunter (Prestwick St. Nicholas)
196 Alex Smith (Bruntsfield)
232 William Steel (Bruntsfield)

Below Nick Faldo after winning his second Open in 1990.

THE
JUBILEE OF THE GOLFING CHAMPIONSHIP
·1860–1910·

THE GREAT TRIUMVIRATE

The
GOLFING DIPLOMA
Presented to
Score
Date
Golf Club

Above The Great Triumvirate of J. H. Taylor, James Braid, and Harry Vardon. Between them they won the British Open 16 times.

THE OPEN'S GREATEST CHAMPIONS

Wins	Player	Nationality	Years
6	Harry Vardon	GB	1896, 1898-99, 1903, 1911, 1914
5	James Braid	GB	1901, 1905-06, 1908, 1910
5	John H. Taylor	GB	1894-95, 1900, 1909, 1913
5	Peter Thomson	Aus	1954-56, 1958, 1965
5	Tom Watson	USA	1975, 1977, 1980, 1982-83
4	Tom Morris, Sr.	GB	1861-62, 1864, 1867
4	Tom Morris, Jr.	GB	1868-70, 1872
4	Willie Park, Sr.	GB	1860, 1863, 1866, 1875
4	Walter Hagen	USA	1922, 1924, 1928-29
4	Bobby Locke	SA	1949-50, 1952, 1957

did keep it. The following year, without a trophy to offer, there was no championship until it was revived in 1872 when Young Tom lifted the new silver claret jug which, today, remains one of the most sought-after trophies in world golf.

Having organized the first eleven competitions, the Prestwick club was finding it increasingly difficult to organize the event as the number of competitors grew and its popularity attracted more spectators. Consequently, the Royal and Ancient at St. Andrews and the Honourable Company of Edinburgh Golfers, based at Musselburgh, shared the organization and took it in turn to play hosts.

All Open courses are links, and in 1894 the competition moved out of Scotland for the first time when Sandwich, in Kent, southern England, played host.

The first Open in England heralded the start of a domination of the championship by three men: John H. Taylor, James Braid, and Harry Vardon. Known as The Great Triumvirate, they captured 16 of the next 21 Opens.

After World War I the switch in dominance moved from British players to American ones, and the breakthrough came in 1921 when Jock Hutchison became the first man to take the trophy across the Atlantic.

The 1920s and 30s was a golden age for American golfers with Jim Barnes, Walter Hagen, Tommy Armour, Gene Sarazen, and Denny Shute all capturing the title. And there was also the world's greatest ever amateur golfer, Robert Tyre "Bobby" Jones, who won the Open three times between 1926 and 1930. The latter year was a remarkable

one for the Georgia lawyer; he captured the Opens, as well as the amateur titles, of both Britain and the US.

The early post-war years belonged to Commonwealth golfers Bobby Locke of South Africa and Australia's Peter Thomson, who won nine titles between them, with Thomson's five wins being the best haul since the days of Taylor, Braid, and Vardon.

Sadly, American interest declined in the 1950s, but Arnold Palmer set about maintaining the British Open's stature as the world's leading golf tournament, and his arrival on the scene aroused great interest in the game in general. He also made sure that many top Americans made the trip across the Atlantic to the UK every summer. Palmer was rewarded with successive titles in 1961 and 1962.

Palmer's arrival on British shores also signaled the birth of the next golfing triumvirate as he, compatriot Jack Nicklaus, and Gary Player of South Africa became great favorites with the British fans. They won eight British Open titles between them; Player doing so in three different decades, the 1950s, 60s, and 70s.

Britain had a rare moment of glory when Tony Jacklin ended an 18-year drought in 1969 by taking

the title from the left-handed New Zealander Bob Charles at Lytham. The Americans continued to dominate the British Tour, with Tom Watson winning a modern record of five titles, but the 1980s saw a switch away from the Americans as first Sandy Lyle, and then Nick Faldo put the trophy back in British hands. Nick Faldo retained the trophy three times.

Spain has also enjoyed her moment of glory, thanks to Severiano Ballesteros's three titles and, in recent years, Greg Norman and Ian Baker-Finch have brought Australia back to the forefront of world golf.

THE OPEN COURSES

Course (Country)	Times used	First used	Last used
Prestwick (Scotland)	24	1860	1925
St. Andrews (Scotland)	24	1873	1990
Muirfield (Scotland)	14	1892	1992
Sandwich (England)	11	1894	1985
Hoylake (England)	10	1897	1967
Lytham (England)	8	1926	1988
Birkdale (England)	7	1954	1991
Musselburgh (Scotland)	6	1874	1889
Troon (Scotland)	6	1923	1989
Carnoustie (Scotland)	5	1931	1975
Deal (England)	2	1909	1920
Turnberry (Scotland)	2	1977	1986
Prince's (England)	1	1932	1932
Portrush (N. Ireland)	1	1951	1951

OPEN RECORDS

Lowest 18-hole total:	63	Mark Hayes, Turnberry 1977
	63	Isao Aoki, Muirfield 1980
	63	Greg Norman, Turnberry 1986
	63	Paul Broadhurst, St. Andrews 1990
	63	Jodie Mudd, Birkdale 1991
Lowest 72-hole total:	268	Tom Watson, Turnberry 1977
Oldest winner:	46 yrs. 3 mths.	Tom Morris, Sr., 1867
Youngest winner:	17 yrs. 8 mths.	Tom Morris, Jr., 1868

TURNBERRY 1977 - RECORDS GALORE

Turnberry, situated on the west coast of Scotland against the beautiful scenic backdrop of Ailsa Craig, the Mull of Kintyre, and the Isle of Arran, was a long time in being added to the list of British Open courses. But when it did arrive in 1977, it was the scene of record scoring, the likes of which had not been seen before.

The Open record for 72 holes previously stood at 276, courtesy of Messrs. Palmer and Weiskopf. But the first two men home at Turnberry covered the 6,875-yard Ailsa course in 268 and 269 respectively, with the champion Tom Watson lowering the Championship record by eight strokes.

The opening round belonged to John Schroeder, son of the 1949 Wimbledon singles champion Ted Schroeder, who shot an opening 66 to take the lead. But he took a back seat on day two as America's Mark Hayes became the first man to shoot a 63 in the Open and thus lower the old record by two strokes, which had stood since Henry Cotton shot the first 65 way back in 1934.

While Hayes was setting his record-breaking round, the big guns of Tom Watson and Jack Nicklaus (pictured above) were making their way up the leader board. They both had third round 65s, after each had opening rounds of

68 and 70, and they set up a wonderful final day. The large crowds were not disappointed as both men played memorable golf, with Watson's final round 65 edging out Nicklaus by one stroke.

In addition to Hayes' record 63, and Watson's four round record 268, Watson's 130 for the last two rounds was a record, his 200 for the last 54 holes was also a record, and he and Nicklaus shared the record low score for the first 54 holes. The crowd of 92,000 was also a record for a Scottish course. Turnberry's first Open was certainly a record-breaking one!

UNITED STATES OPEN

THE FORERUNNER OF the US Open took place in 1894 when Willie Dunn won a match-play event. However, the first championship carrying the US Open name was held at Newport, Rhode Island, on October 4, 1895. It was scheduled for the previous month, but clashed with the America's Cup yacht race, which was taking place in Rhode Island at the same time.

The first Open was over four rounds of Newport's 9-hole course, and the winner from a field of ten professionals and one amateur was English-born Horace Rawlins, who took the first prize of $150 with a 36-hole total of 173.

The first 16 Opens were all won by British-born golfers, and when Harry Vardon made the journey across the Atlantic to take the title in 1900, he did a great deal to help popularize the game in the U.S.

In 1911, a home-bred player captured the title for the first time when Johnny McDermott won a three-way playoff.

McDermott retained his title in 1912, and the following year, victory by an unknown amateur

changed the course of golfing history in the United States.

Twenty-year-old Francis Ouimet lived across the road from the Brookline Country Club, venue for the 1913 Open. He entered the competition without realistically expecting to have any impact on the big names of the world of professional golf, including Britain's top golfers Vardon and Ted Ray.

But what a memorable occasion it was as Ouimet shared the lead after 72 holes and then went on to beat the Britons by five and six strokes respectively in the playoff. The British domination of world golf was over for 70 years, give or take the odd blip.

Ted Ray took the title back to Britain in 1920, but that was the last time until Tony Jacklin's success in 1970. Since then, no Briton has captured the US title, and Australia's David Graham in 1981 was the only foreigner to break the American stranglehold.

Bobby Jones, Ben Hogan, and Jack Nicklaus, three of the biggest names in world golf, have all won the Open four times. Hogan's 1950 success, less than two years after a near-fatal car accident, was one of the most emotional in the tournament's long history.

Above Bobby Jones (right) after completing the game's most remarkable Grand Slam in 1930.

Left Britain's Ted Ray, the 1920 US Open winner.

SAM SNEAD'S CATALOGUE OF NEAR MISSES

In terms of wins, Sam Snead is the most successful golfer in US history, with 81 Tour wins during his long career. But, remarkably, the man who has won seven Majors has never won the US Open. Even more surprising, he finished second in his very first Open in 1937, and many thought that after such a start the title would be a formality one day. But it was not to be.

These are Sam Snead's near misses in the US Open.

1937 Oakland Hills, Michigan

281	Ralph Guldahl	71	69	72	69
283	Sam Snead	69	73	70	71
285	Bobby Cruickshank	73	73	67	72

1947 St Louis, Missouri

282	Lew Worsham	70	70	71	71
282	Sam Snead	72	70	70	70

Worsham won play-off 69-70

285	Bobby Locke	68	74	70	73
285	Porky Oliver	73	70	71	71

1949 Medinah, Illinois

286	Cary Middlecoff	75	67	69	75
287	Sam Snead	73	73	71	70
287	Clayton Heafner	72	71	71	73

1953 Oakmont, Pennsylvania

283	Ben Hogan	67	72	73	71
289	Sam Snead	72	69	72	76
292	Lloyd Mangrum	73	70	74	75

The nearest Snead came was in 1947. He holed an 18-foot putt on the 72nd hole to force the play-off with Worsham. But on the same hole in the play-off he missed from less than a yard, and lost by one stroke.

Above "She's all mine." Curtis Strange after capturing his first US Open title in 1988. He won the title again in 1989 to become the first back-to-back winner since Ben Hogan in 1951.

Left Sam Snead in action during the first post-war British Open, at St. Andrews in 1946. He won the title from Bobby Locke and Johnny Bulla, but he never captured the US title.

OPEN RECORDS

Lowest 18-hole total: 63 Johnny Miller, Oakmont 1973
63 Tom Weiskopf, Baltusrol 1980
63 Jack Nicklaus, Baltusrol 1980
Lowest 72-hole total: 272 Jack Nicklaus, Baltusrol 1980
Oldest winner: 45 yrs Hale Irwin, 1990
Youngest winner: 19 yrs 10 mths Johnny McDermott, 1911

US MASTERS

THE MASTERS IS the youngest of the four Majors. It is the only one that is invitation only, and the only one played on the same course each year - the wonderful setting of the Augusta National course in Georgia.

The Masters and the Augusta National were the brainchild of Bobby Jones. The course was designed and constructed by Alister Mackenzie on a site that was formerly a nursery, and the reminder of its former days is evident in the abundance of beautiful shrubs, bushes, trees, and flowers that line the course. Each hole is named after the plant life adjacent to it.

The first Masters, back in 1934, attracted very little interest, and in an effort to arouse media attention Bobby Jones came out of retirement. The first winner was Horton Smith, who snatched a last-gasp win from Craig Wood, thanks to finishing birdie-par.

Wood was again runner-up the second year after losing a playoff to Gene Sarazen, whose double eagle at the par-5 15th is one of golf's most talked-about shots.

To win the coveted green jacket that is presented to the Masters champion each year requires the highest concentration because the course, with its narrow fairways and abundance of bunkers and water, poses the sternest of tests. One man who has passed that test - not once, but a staggering six

Above The US Masters Trophy.

Below left Severiano Ballesteros putting to win in 1980.

Below right Nick Price shooting a Masters record 63 in 1986.

MASTERS RECORDS		
Lowest 18-hole total:	63	Nick Price, 1986
Lowest 72-hole total:	271	Jack Nicklaus, 1965
	271	Ray Floyd, 1976
Oldest winner:	46 yrs 2 mths	Jack Nicklaus, 1986
Youngest winner:	23 yrs 0 mths	Seve Ballesteros, 1980

times - is Jack Nicklaus, the "Master of Augusta." His sixth victory came at the age of 46.

Gary Player was the first non-American winner of the Masters in 1961, and he won it on two more occasions, but no other non-American won until Severiano Ballesteros took the title in 1980. This heralded the start of a European domination which shook the American golfing world. Ballesteros won again in 1983. Germany's Bernhard Langer won in 1985, and between 1988 and 1991 British players won four consecutive titles, thanks to Sandy Lyle, Ian Woosnam, and Nick Faldo, who emulated the great Jack Nicklaus by winning back-to-back titles. Fred Couples, however, arrested the situation in 1992 by recapturing the title for the home players.

JACK NICKLAUS - THE MASTER OF AUGUSTA

Jack Nicklaus has won the Masters a record six times. These are details of his wins:

1963

| 286 | Jack Nicklaus | 74 | 66 | 74 | 72 |
| 287 | Tony Lema | 74 | 69 | 74 | 70 |

1965

271	Jack Nicklaus	67	71	64	69
280	Arnold Palmer	70	68	72	70
280	Gary Player	65	73	69	73

1966

288	Jack Nicklaus	68	76	72	72
288	Tommy Jacobs	75	71	70	72
288	Gay Brewer	74	72	72	70

Nicklaus won play-off 70-72-78

1972

286	Jack Nicklaus	68	71	73	74
289	Tom Weiskopf	74	71	70	74
289	Bruce Crampton	72	75	69	73
289	Bobby Mitchell	73	72	71	73

1975

276	Jack Nicklaus	68	67	73	68
277	Johnny Miller	75	71	65	66
277	Tom Weiskopf	69	72	66	70

1986

279	Jack Nicklaus	74	71	69	65
280	Greg Norman	70	72	68	70
280	Tom Kite	70	74	68	68

In addition to his six wins Nicklaus finished second or joint second four times, in 1964, 1971, 1977, 1981. Right, Langer helps Nicklaus don the coveted green jacket in 1986.

THE US PGA CHAMPIONSHIP

THE LEAST PRESTIGIOUS of the four Majors, the US PGA Championship, is nevertheless a trophy much sought by American golfers. Qualification for the PGA Championship is based on performances on the US Tour which, effectively, makes it a very American event. To date, only Gary Player of South Africa, Nick Price of Zimbabwe, and the Australian pair of David Graham and Wayne Grady have been non-American winners.

The first PGA Championship was in 1916, the year of the formation of the US Professional Golfers Association. One of the biggest attractions of winning the Championship, apart from the large check that accompanies success, is future exemption from pre-qualifying for all US Tour events.

From its inauguration until 1958, the Championship was a match-play event, and in the 1920s Walter Hagen proved himself to be one of the finest exponents of this form of golf by taking the title five times in the seven years between 1921 and 1927. Between 1924 and

Above John Daly, the big-hitting surprise winner of the US PGA Championship in 1991.

Right Paul Runyan (center), winner of the 1938 PGA Championship, receives his trophy after beating Sam Snead (looking on, left) in the final at Shawnee Country Club.

WALTER HAGEN – THE MATCHPLAY EXPERT

Between 1921 and 1927 Walter Hagen competed in six of the seven US PGA Championships that were held. He won five of the six in which he competed and was beaten finalist in the other. This is his amazing record.

1921 Inwood, New York
Final: Walter Hagen beat Jim Barnes 3 & 2

1922 Oakmont, Pennsylvania
Did not compete

1923 Pelham, New York
Final: Gene Sarazen beat Walter Hagen at 38th hole

1924 French Lick, Indiana
Final: Walter Hagen beat Jim Barnes 2 up

1925 Olympia Fields, Illinois
Final: Walter Hagen beat Bill Melhorn 6 & 5

1926 Salisbury, New York
Final: Walter Hagen beat Leo Diegel 5 & 3

1927 Cedar Crest, Texas
Final: Walter Hagen beat Joe Turnesa 1 up

His run of 22 consecutive wins came to an end in the quarter-final in 1928 when beaten by Leo Diegel.

1928, when he lost in the quarter-finals, Hagen went 22 consecutive matches without defeat against the cream of the professionals. When he lost, the PGA asked him for the trophy back, and he replied that he had left it in the back of a taxi a couple of years earlier! The trophy was eventually recovered.

In 1980 Jack Nicklaus equaled Hagen's record of five wins. But it is the one Major that Arnold Palmer never captured.

For drama, the final of the 1930 Championship between Gene Sarazen and Tommy Armour takes some beating. The two stalwarts engaged in a wonderfully close battle for 35 holes. At the last, Armour holed a putt from 14 feet. Sarazen then had a similar putt, but missed by inches, and with it went his chance at the title.

Now a medal-play event, like the other Majors, the PGA has a regular August date each year and is the last of the season's four Majors. At one time it used to either clash with, or be played within a week of, the British Open, and for this reason Ben Hogan was deprived of the chance of winning all four Majors in 1953.

PGA RECORDS

Lowest 18-hole total:	63	Bruce Crampton, Firestone 1975
	63	Ray Floyd, Southern Hills 1982
	63	Gary Player, Shoal Creek 1984
Lowest 72-hole total:	271	Bobby Nichols, Columbus 1964
Oldest winner:	48 yrs 5 mths	Julius Boros, 1968
Youngest winner:	20 yrs 6 mths	Gene Sarazen, 1922

RYDER CUP

THE WORLD'S LEADING professional team tournament, the Ryder Cup, has aroused a great deal of interest on both sides of the Atlantic in recent years, particularly as the American domination which lasted over 20 years eventually came to an end in the 1980s. For the first time since the Cup's early days, it is no longer a one-sided affair.

The forerunner of the Ryder Cup was a match between professional teams from Britain and the United States at Wentworth in 1926. The British team won 13½ to 1½. This match led to English seed merchant Samuel Ryder suggesting a biennial tournament between the two nations, held alternately on each side of the Atlantic. And so the Ryder Cup was born, with the first official match taking place at Worcester, Massachusetts, on June 3-4, 1927.

Ryder's interest in golf started when he suffered ill-health while living in Hertfordshire, England. Upon the suggestion of a local minister, the Reverend Frank Wheeler, he joined the St. Albans

Left The most famous international golfing team trophy, the Ryder Cup.

Below Walter Hagen holds the trophy after the USA won the first Ryder Cup in 1927.

Verulam Golf Club, and suddenly golf became his enduring passion.

He befriended some of the day's great golfers, Braid, Taylor, Vardon, and local professional Abe Mitchell. The statue on top of the Ryder Cup trophy is modeled on Mitchell.

The Americans won the first Ryder Cup, Britain won the next on home soil, and so it went for the first four times, with the home team winning on each occasion. But that all changed in 1937 when the Americans won on British soil for the first time, winning 8-4 at Southport & Ainsdale. Britain did not gain their next win until 1957, skippered by Dai Rees, and for the next two decades, the Americans dominated.

The competition became too one-sided, with the British team suffering some heavy defeats. In an attempt to arrest the decline of

Above Opposing captains J. H. Taylor (left) and Walter Hagen shake hands before the 1933 Ryder Cup at Southport & Ainsdale. Samuel Ryder is in the middle.

Below A joyous Dai Rees after Britain won the Ryder Cup in 1957.

the competition, it was agreed that from 1979 European golfers could compete. And America's opponents became Europe instead of Great Britain and Ireland.

The Americans continued to take charge until 1983, when the Europeans, under new captain Tony Jacklin, came within a point of their first win since 1957. Two years later at The Belfry, Jacklin enjoyed one of his finest moments

when he led the side to victory, thus ending a 28-year drought. But more was to come as Jacklin and his men retained the trophy two years later and thus became the first team to defeat the Americans on home soil.

By now, interest in the Ryder Cup was greater than ever, and back at The Belfry in 1989, an intense battle resulted in a tied Cup, only the second ever, but, as

defending champions, the Europeans managed to keep their hands on the trophy. In 1991, however, the Americans wrested it back. But the days are gone when the Americans could be assured of holding onto it, and the hype surrounding the event every two years makes the Ryder Cup one of the great occasions on the golfing calendar.

Below A delighted European team after winning the 1989 Ryder Cup . . . they retained the trophy after they tied 14-14 at The Belfry.

Bottom right Tony Jacklin savors one of the greatest moments in his career after guiding the European team to their first Ryder Cup success in 1985, inflicting the first defeat on the Americans in 28 years.

THE RYDER CUP 1985 EUROPEAN TEAM

After 28 years, the European team, under Tony Jacklin, managed to wrest the Ryder Cup from the American grip in 1985, winning by five points at the Belfry. This is how it was done.
European names first

DAY ONE
Foursomes
Severiano Ballesteros & Manuel Pinero beat Curtis Strange & Mark O'Meara 2 & 1
Bernhard Langer & Nick Faldo lost to Calvin Peete & Tom Kite 3 & 2
Sandy Lyle & Ken Brown lost to Lanny Wadkins & Ray Floyd 4 & 3
Howard Clark & Sam Torrance lost to Craig Stadler & Hal Sutton 3 & 2
Score: Europe 1 UNITED STATES 3

Four-balls
Paul Way & Ian Woosnam beat Fuzzy Zoeller & Hubert Green 1 hole
Severiano Ballesteros & Manuel Pinero beat Andy North & Peter Jacobsen 2 & 1
Bernhard Langer & José Maria Canizares halved with Craig Stadler & Hal Sutton
Sam Torrance & Howard Clark lost to Ray Floyd & Lanny Wadkins 1 hole
Score: Europe 3½ UNITED STATES 4½

DAY TWO
Four-balls
Sam Torrance & Howard Clark beat Tom Kite & Andy North 2 & 1
Paul Way & Ian Woosnam beat Hubert Green & Fuzzy Zoeller 4 & 3
Severiano Ballesteros & Manuel Pinero lost to Mark O'Meara & Lanny Wadkins 3 & 2
Bernhard Langer & Sandy Lyle halved with Curtis Strange & Craig Stadler
Score: Europe 6 United States 6

Foursomes
José Maria Canizares & José Rivero beat Tom Kite & Calvin Peete 7 & 5
Severiano Ballesteros & Manuel Pinero beat Craig Stadler & Hal Sutton 5 & 4
Paul Way & Ian Woosnam lost to Curtis Strange & Peter Jacobsen 4 & 2
Bernhard Langer & Ken Brown beat Ray Floyd & Lanny Wadkins 3 & 2
Score: EUROPE 9 United States 7

DAY THREE
Singles
Manuel Pinero beat Lanny Wadkins 3 & 1
Ian Woosnam lost to Craig Stadler 2 & 1
Paul Way beat Ray Floyd 2 holes
Severiano Ballesteros halved with Tom Kite
Sandy Lyle beat Peter Jacobsen 3 & 2
Bernhard Langer beat Hal Sutton 5 & 4
Sam Torrance beat Andy North 1 hole
Howard Clark beat Mark O'Meara 1 hole
José Rivero lost to Calvin Peete 1 hole
Nick Faldo lost to Hubert Green 3 & 1
José Maria Canizares beat Fuzzy Zoeller 2 holes
Ken Brown lost to Curtis Strange 4 & 2
FINAL SCORE: EUROPE 16½ United States 11½

BELL'S SCOTCH
RYDER CUP

WORLD MATCHPLAY CHAMPIONSHIP

capturing the title five times between 1965 and 1973. His record of five wins was equaled by Spain's Severiano Ballesteros in 1991.

One of the most memorable moments of the World Matchplay was in 1979 when Japan's Isao Aoki, the eventual beaten finalist, holed-in-one at the second. His feat won him a furnished

Left Arnold Palmer, winner of the first World Matchplay title in 1964.

Below The "Master of Wentworth," Gary Player after beating Graham Marsh to win his fifth World Matchplay title in 1973.

MATCHPLAY GOLF IS very popular at club level, but among professionals it is played in a small handful of major competitions. The Ryder Cup, of course, is all played to matchplay rules, but the world's leading individual tournament is unquestionably the World Matchplay Championship played at Wentworth each October. It is an invitational event with golfers from around the world taking part.

First held in 1964, it was originally sponsored by Piccadilly, who remained with the event until 1977 when succeeded by Colgate. Between 1979 and 1990, the sponsor was Suntory, and since 1991 has been the Japanese car manufacturer Toyota.

Arnold Palmer was the inaugural champion, beating Britain's Neil Coles in the first final. Britain had to wait until 1987 for her first champion, when Ian Woosnam beat fellow Briton Sandy Lyle in the final.

Gary Player was the master of matchplay in the 1960s and 70s,

apartment overlooking the Wentworth course.

HOW IT IS PLAYED

Twelve invited players take part each year with four receiving "top seed status." Those four do not take part in the first round and "receive a bye" into the second. The other eight fight it out on a straight knockout basis. The four winners then join the four seeds in the second round, and it continues as a knockout tournament. Matches are over 36 holes. If a match is not resolved after two complete rounds, it is decided on a "sudden death" basis.

Above Ian Woosnam looks delighted with his 1987 Suntory Trophy.

Right Seve Ballesteros at the 1991 World Matchplay.

WOMEN'S MAJORS

THERE ARE FOUR women's Majors, and all four are played in the United States.

The most prestigious is the US WOMEN'S OPEN, inaugurated in 1946, four years before the formation of the US LPGA. The first winner was Patty Berg who beat Betty Jameson 5 and 4 in the final on the only occasion it was played under match-play rules. Mickey Wright and Betsy Rawls both won the Open a record four times.

The LPGA CHAMPIONSHIP was first held in 1955 and, like the Open, was a match-play event in its first year and was won by Beverly Hanson. Mickey Wright, with four wins, has been the most successful golfer in LPGA championships.

The DU MAURIER CLASSIC started life as the La Canadienne in 1973 and was known as the Peter Jackson Classic between 1974 and 1982. During that time it was also granted Major status, in 1979, and won by Amy Alcott. Pat Bradley, in 1980, 1985 and 1986, has won it a record three times.

The newest of the four Majors is the NABISCO DINAH SHORE, which was designated a Major in 1983 after changing its name from the Colgate-Dinah Shore, which had been inaugurated in 1972. The first winner of the event as a Major was Amy Alcott, who won it for a record third time in 1991.

One of the most successful lady golfers in the 1980s was America's Amy Alcott. She won three Majors during the decade, including the 1980 US Women's Open.

Right American Nancy Lopez has been successful on both sides of the Atlantic. She is seen here after capturing the 1979 LPGA title at Sunningdale, England.

Below Pat Bradley, winner of the du Maurier Classic a record three times between 1980 and 1986, including back-to-back wins in '85 and '86.

DID YOU KNOW?

The highest score ever recorded for a single hole is 166, achieved over 80 years ago by a woman player from Pennsylvania. Many of the strokes were made from a rowing boat while her ball floated a mile and a half down a river.

THE WORLD'S OUTSTANDING GOLF COURSES

GOLF IS BLESSED with so many wonderful golf courses that it is difficult to know where in the world to begin. So we'll take the uncontroversial way out and present them in alphabetical order by country as follows:

AUSTRALIA
CANADA
EIRE
ENGLAND
FRANCE
NORTHERN IRELAND
PORTUGAL
SCOTLAND
SPAIN
SWITZERLAND
UNITED STATES

Each entry includes a map of the course showing bunkers, water hazards, fairways, clubhouse, and numbered tees, as well as pictures of the course and a scorecard.

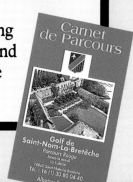

ROYAL MELBOURNE

ONE OF THE finest golf courses outside Britain or the United States is the Royal Melbourne Club in Australia, which has continuous membership dating from July 1891.

The official outfit for all members in those early days was a scarlet coat with gold buttons, knickers, and a Tam O'Shanter to confirm the club's Scottish connection.

The course moved to the Sandringham district of Melbourne in 1901, and a new course was laid out. Its deep bunkers turned it into one of the great championship courses in the world.

While retaining some characteristics of Scottish links, it also has some of the beauty of the Augusta National course. But that is hardly surprising, because the man hired by Bobby Jones to

design Augusta, Alister Mackenzie, was hired to design the new course at Melbourne in the 1920s. The East Course was added in 1932, and the original course was named the West Course.

Such is the design of the two that holes from both can be incorporated into one 18-hole course for major championships.

The greens at Melbourne are lifted every six years to guarantee their trueness, and, consequently, they are lightning fast.

For a true test of a golfer's ability and nerve, the 6th and 14th holes provide a daunting task. Both are doglegs; the first requires the decision to play short of, or attempt to negotiate, some awkwardly placed bunkers. The latter is a 90-degree dogleg, but trees lining the right-hand side of the fairway make it difficult to assess the correct line.

Right The fabulous setting of the 5th hole on Royal Melbourne's West Course.

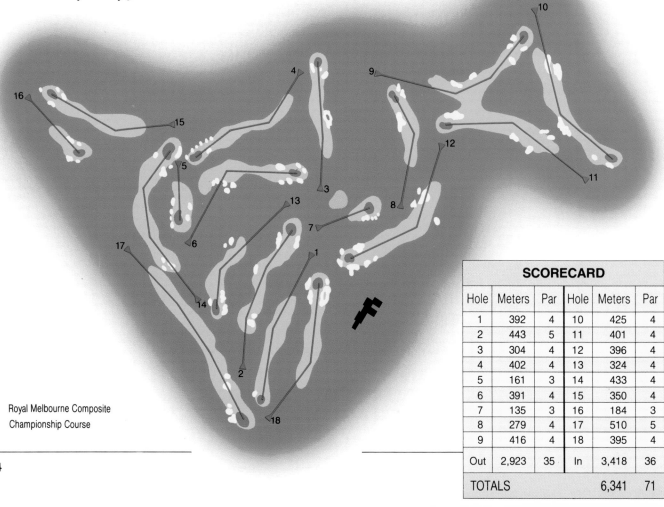

Royal Melbourne Composite
Championship Course

SCORECARD					
Hole	Meters	Par	Hole	Meters	Par
1	392	4	10	425	4
2	443	5	11	401	4
3	304	4	12	396	4
4	402	4	13	324	4
5	161	3	14	433	4
6	391	4	15	350	4
7	135	3	16	184	3
8	279	4	17	510	5
9	416	4	18	395	4
Out	2,923	35	In	3,418	36
TOTALS				6,341	71

GLEN ABBEY

SITUATED AT OAKVILLE, Ontario, Glen Abbey became the home of the Canadian Open in 1977 and, except for 1980, has been its permanent home ever since.

The course was one of the first to be purpose-built to meet the demands of modern-day golf in the 1970s, when Jack Nicklaus was asked to design a course taking in Sixteen Mile Creek close to Lake Ontario.

It is a spectacular course, and Nicklaus took full advantage of the natural beauty of the area. Such is the appeal of the place that the Golf House, formerly a Jesuit retreat, is the home of the Royal Canadian Golf Association.

Nicklaus designed the course with the spectator in mind, and banked areas behind the greens are a feature. Also, many of the greens and tees are within close proximity of the clubhouse.

Huge crowds attend the Canadian Open each year, regarded by many as the fifth major, and the large areas between the fairways help lessen the problem of crowd congestion that happens at many golf courses.

Nicklaus was not left to start from scratch, because there had been a course on the site since the

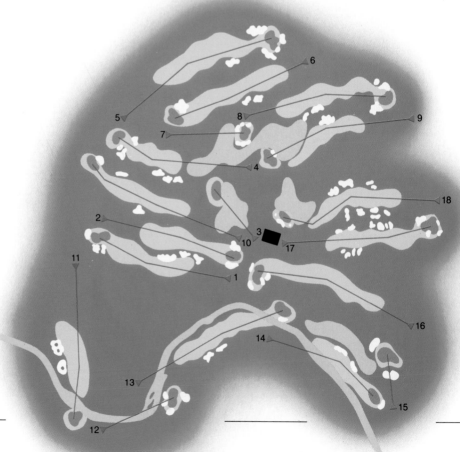

SCORECARD					
Hole	Yards	Par	Hole	Yards	Par
1	369	4	10	435	5
2	380	4	11	426	4
3	123	3	12	152	3
4	345	4	13	481	5
5	452	5	14	330	4
6	395	4	15	115	3
7	135	3	16	452	5
8	391	4	17	365	4
9	383	4	18	461	5
Out	2,973	35	In	3,217	38
TOTALS				6,190	73

early 1960s when the Jesuits sold the land. But Nicklaus's task was a major rebuilding one.

The natural terrain of the ravine has been fully utilized and the 11th to 15th holes, known as the Valley, are the toughest on the course. The short 15th, although only 140 yards from the back tee, is extremely tough. The green slopes from back to front but bunkers at back and front make correct club selection crucial.

The course opened in June 1976 when designer Nicklaus played an exhibition match with the reigning Canadian Open champion Tom Weiskopf.

Left Glen Abbey's 13th.

Below What a closing hole! The 18th at Glen Abbey. Even Lawrence of Arabia wouldn't have survived in that.

DID YOU KNOW?

There have been some notable golf non-enthusiasts as the following quotes reveal: "An expensive way of playing marbles," G. K. Chesterton. "An ineffectual attempt to direct an uncontrollable sphere into an inaccessible hole with instruments ill-adapted to the purpose," Sir Winston Churchill. "A good walk spoiled," Mark Twain.

THE NATIONAL

ALREADY THE NATIONAL is regarded as one of the top Canadian golf courses, even though it was only constructed in 1973.

The course was designed by Tom Fazio, nephew of the former professional and course designer George Fazio, who offered plenty of advice to his nephew during the construction of the National.

The idea of a course at Woodbridge, Ontario, came from car parts manufacturer Gil Blechman, who was fed up with the way of life in suburban Toronto golf and country clubs. He decided it was time to build a "proper" golf club and he set about fulfilling that dream. His instructions to Fazio were simple: "Build me the best golf course in the world."

The site for the new course was Pine Valley, which was already laid out for golf, but it had nothing like the splendor of its New Jersey namesake. The Pine Valley course was not totally suitable, but when Fazio spotted some adjacent land, he knew that Blechman's dream could be realized.

The additional land gave an extra five holes. They are regarded as the toughest in the whole of Canada, but Fazio also managed to incorporate some majestic scenery into them.

Although completed in 1973, the National Golf Club was not officially opened for play until 1975. Blechman's idea of building a golf course without the other distractions of the "country club atmosphere" are clearly visible at the National. Golf is what the National is for, nothing else.

Water hazards affect nine of the 18 holes, and the outward nine are long and tough, with the wind making them even more difficult on certain days. Because of the natural terrain, the back nine holes are situated some 100 feet below the front nine, and the natural hills make it possible for more than 50,000 spectators to fill the course at any one time.

One of the finest testaments to the National's design came shortly after it was opened, when all the players in a tournament for leading local amateurs were asked to name the best hole on the course. The result showed 14 different answers.

SCORECARD					
Hole	Yards	Par	Hole	Yards	Par
1	388	4	10	176	3
2	427	4	11	406	4
3	424	4	12	503	5
4	581	5	13	379	4
5	205	3	14	421	4
6	531	5	15	221	3
7	445	4	16	384	4
8	190	3	17	428	4
9	425	4	18	455	5
Out	3,616	36	In	3,373	36
TOTALS				6,989	72

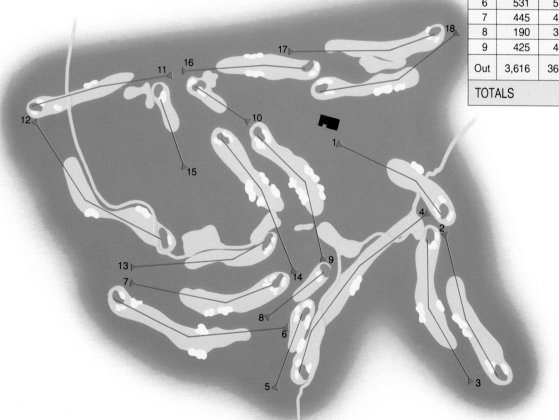

Above The 13th at the National is well guarded by greenside bunkers.

Right . . . and so is the 10th.

BALLYBUNION

SET AMONG SUCH beauty and splendor, the natural assets of the Kerry coast have been fully utilized in designing and building the course. Its admirers have described Ballybunion as "the best golf course in the world." That is a bold claim, but there is no doubting its standing as one of the truly great links courses.

Situated on the Atlantic coast of the Republic of Ireland in County Kerry, the course commands beautiful views out to the ocean and is a very popular course with British and European golfers.

Many of the holes, particularly those alongside the edge of the ocean, are lined with huge sandhills which give the feeling of playing in a vast amphitheater.

The club dates to 1893, but after five years it folded following financial difficulties. However, it was re-formed in 1906 by a retired Indian Army officer, Colonel Bartholomew, and a few friends. They brought in Lionel Hewson to lay out a new nine-hole course. It was not until 1927 that it became a full 18-hole course, but by the 1930s it had become a championship course when Betty Lachford won the Irish Ladies title there.

A new clubhouse was built in

Set on the Atlantic coast of eastern Ireland, Ballybunion's Old Course is a testing links course.

1971, and the order of the holes was changed that same year, with play starting at what was the original 14th hole.

Uphill, downhill, and sideway lies among the undulating terrain do make Ballybunion a difficult course, but a look around confirms it as one of the most beautiful.

SCORECARD					
Hole	Yards	Par	Hole	Yards	Par
1	392	4	10	359	4
2	445	4	11	449	4
3	220	3	12	192	3
4	498	5	13	484	5
5	508	5	14	131	3
6	364	4	15	216	3
7	423	4	16	490	5
8	153	3	17	385	4
9	454	4	18	379	4
Out	3,457	36	In	3,085	35
TOTALS				6,542	71

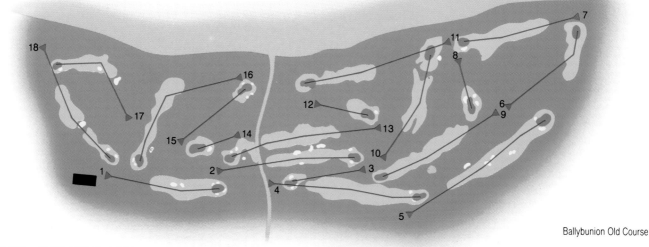

Ballybunion Old Course

PORTMARNOCK

ONE OF THE venues for the Irish Open, Portmarnock played host to the very first championship in 1927, won by George Duncan with a score of 312.

Situated in Co. Dublin, Portmarnock is not one of the most spectacular Irish golf courses, but certainly rates as one of the "greats." Bobby Locke, that great South African golfer, once rated it among the best in Europe.

The site for the course was found by accident. Two men, named Ross and Pickeman, came across the expanse of land while out in a boat in 1893. Access to the land was solely by boat. However, the two intrepid explorers took a fancy to the land, and by the end of the year they had formed a golf club.

Apart from playing host to the Irish Open, Portmarnock has staged the British Amateur Championship, and in 1960 Arnold Palmer made his first appearance in Europe when he played in the winning United States World Cup team alongside Sam Snead.

For many years the Portmarnock professional was Harry Bradshaw.

Although not a venue for the British Open, Portmarnock in Co. Dublin has staged many major championships including the British Amateur Championship and the World Cup.

SCORECARD

Hole	Meters	Par	Hole	Meters	Par
1	358	4	10	341	4
2	346	4	11	389	4
3	351	4	12	136	3
4	407	4	13	516	5
5	364	4	14	359	4
6	550	5	15	191	3
7	161	3	16	484	5
8	368	4	17	423	4
9	404	4	18	381	4
Out	3,309	36	In	3,220	36
TOTALS				6,529	72

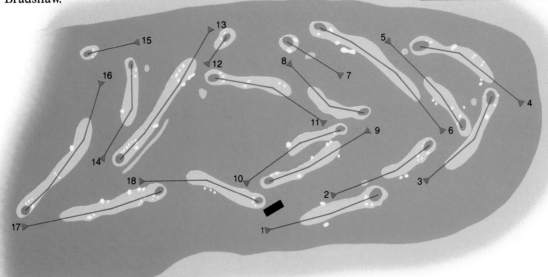

THE BELFRY

HOME OF THE PGA, The Belfry has become one of the best-known courses in Britain in recent years, thanks largely to the mass of publicity given to the two Ryder Cup matches played there in the 1980s.

The first was in 1985 when Tony Jacklin and his gallant men became the first to beat the American team since 1957, and four years later they retained the trophy after a thrilling tie.

The Belfry was designed to be the British equivalent of Augusta, home of the US Masters. And while it certainly boasts some beautifully scenic holes and attractive plant life, it has not quite recaptured the beauty of Augusta.

It was transformed from potato fields in the English Midlands to a top-class golf course by designers Dave Thomas and Peter Alliss, and in 1977 it opened its doors for the first time. There are two courses, the Derby Course and the larger Brabazon Course, which is used for major events.

The designers, in an attempt to give it a more American look, made water a major feature. And the 18th hole is one of the most picturesque in British golf. It requires two shots over water to the pin 474 yards away. The 10th is also very Americanized, with the green guarded by a large lake. The big hitters can reach the green off the tee. The not-so-big, and not-so-fortunate hitters, give their balls an "early bath."

The Hennessy Cognac Cup was the first major tournament at The Belfry, and the State Express Classic and Lawrence Batley Classic also had their homes at this West Midlands course situated near Sutton Coldfield. The English Open is now played here annually.

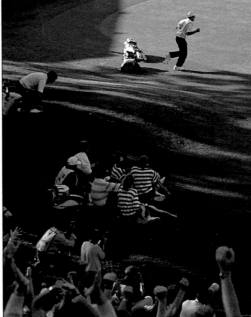

Top The Belfry Clubhouse. One of the finest English courses, The Belfry is now the home of the European PGA.

Above The vast crowds bask in sunshine and glory as the Europeans retained the Ryder Cup after they tied 14-14 in 1989.

Left The Belfry's 10th has shades of Augusta about it, with water being a prominent feature.

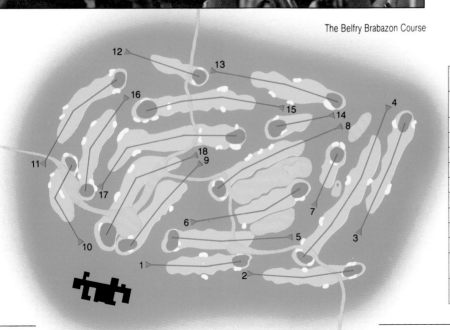

DID YOU KNOW?

Golfing lore says that the word "fore" is believed to come from the military command "Beware before!", used in the 16th century to warn soldiers to fall to the ground to enable friendly gunfire to pass over them. It is believed that the Scottish reformer John Knox first used the term in the 16th century.

The Belfry Brabazon Course

SCORECARD					
Hole	Yards	Par	Hole	Yards	Par
1	418	4	10	275	4
2	349	4	11	420	4
3	465	4	12	235	3
4	579	5	13	394	4
5	399	4	14	194	3
6	396	4	15	550	5
7	183	3	16	410	4
8	460	5	17	575	5
9	400	4	18	474	4
Out	3,649	37	In	3,527	36
TOTALS				7,176	73

ROYAL BIRKDALE

The impressive Royal Birkdale clubhouse.

WITH ITS SPLENDID clubhouse, the Royal Birkdale course on the outskirts of Southport is the finest and best-known course on that part of the Fylde coast, between the Merseyside town and Formby just down the coast.

Birkdale's severe rough makes it a testing course and one that calls for maximum effort from even the most qualified of players. It is regarded as one of the great modern-day championship courses.

The Birkdale club was founded by local enthusiasts in 1889 at a site closer to the town centre, with the Portland Hotel as its headquarters. But it moved to its present-day home about four miles from the town centre in 1897. It underwent major redesign work in 1931 and the clubhouse proudly stands as one of the finest in Britain.

The club was granted Royal patronage in 1951 and three years later it staged its first British Open, when Peter Thomson of Australia triumphed. It has now staged seven Opens, 1991 being the latest occasion that the Championship came to the north-west of England.

Although it has hosted championship golf since before the First World War it was not until after the Second World War that it hosted major international competitions. It has since hosted the Walker Cup, the Curtis Cup and the Ryder Cup, when Britain and the United States fought out a memorable tie here in 1969.

One of the British Open's great golf shots was played from behind a bush by Arnold Palmer at Birkdale's 15th hole (now 16th) on his way to winning his first title in 1961. Despite his lie, he found the green 140 yards away with a six-iron and was left with a 15-foot putt. A plaque has been laid into the fairway close to the spot where he played the magical shot.

The rough and bracken alongside the fairways give an appearance of severity, but it would be accurate to describe the course as "demanding but fair". However, play a wayward shot and it then becomes severe.

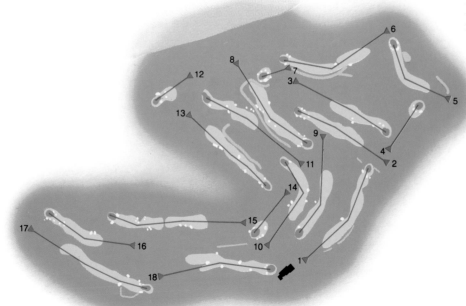

SCORECARD					
Hole	Yards	Par	Hole	Yards	Par
1	448	4	10	395	4
2	417	4	11	409	4
3	409	4	12	184	3
4	203	3	13	475	4
5	346	4	14	199	3
6	473	4	15	543	5
7	156	3	16	414	4
8	458	4	17	525	5
9	414	4	18	472	4
Out	3,324	34	In	3,616	36
TOTALS				6,940	70

Top The plaque alongside Birkdale's 16th fairway to commemorate Arnold Palmer's magical shot in the 1961 Open.

Above Fultom Allem coming out of some of Birkdale's severe rough.

Left A view up Birkdale's 8th fairway.

ROYAL LIVERPOOL

THE ROYAL LIVERPOOL Club is not situated in Liverpool, as its name implies, but is at the end of the Wirral peninsula on the opposite side of the River Mersey at Hoylake.

The club is steeped in golfing history, and, in addition to producing such great champions as John Ball and Harold Hilton, it was responsible for inaugurating many of the great championships which are still played today.

It was host to the first Amateur Championship in 1885, the first English Amateur Championship in 1925, was the venue for the first international match between England and Scotland in 1902, and the first between amateurs of Great Britain and the United States in 1921, the match that was the forerunner of the Walker Cup. Hardly surprisingly, with such a tradition, it has also been home of the British Open ten times between 1897 and 1967. Coincidentally, the first winner at Hoylake was the local amateur Harold Hilton.

The club was formed in 1869 by exiled Scots living in the Liverpool area, who laid out the course on a racecourse owned by the Royal Liverpool Hunt Club. Jack Morris, nephew of Old Tom

Morris, was the club's first professional. The course was increased to its full 18 holes in 1871 and has changed very little since. Many out-of-bounds markers await wayward shots. The 11th hole is named the Alps because it has high sandhills which require a very long carry from the tee.

Right The clubhouse at Royal Liverpool, Hoylake.

Below Greg Norman in action at Hoylake's 11th.

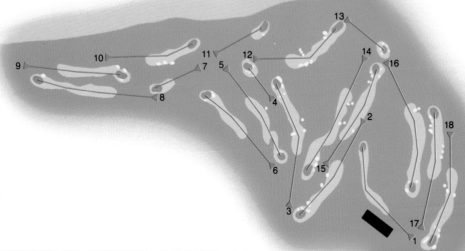

SCORECARD					
Hole	Yards	Par	Hole	Yards	Par
1	428	4	10	409	4
2	429	4	11	200	3
3	505	5	12	454	4
4	195	3	13	157	3
5	449	4	14	516	5
6	423	4	15	460	4
7	200	3	16	560	5
8	519	5	17	418	4
9	393	4	18	395	4
Out	3,541	36	In	3,569	36
TOTALS				7,110	72

ROYAL LYTHAM AND ST. ANNES

THE FYLDE COAST course at Lytham first hosted the British Open in 1926 and was privileged to witness the great American amateur Bobby Jones win his first title. But for sheer nostalgia the 1969 Open took some beating: Tony Jacklin thwarted the challenge of the left-handed New Zealander Bob Charles to become the first British winner since Max Faulkner in 1951.

Lytham has a remarkable record of not having produced an American professional winner of the British Open despite staging the Championship eight times. Since Jones' victory, the other winners, apart from Jacklin, have been Bobby Locke (South Africa), Peter Thomson (Australia), Bob Charles (New Zealand), Gary Player (South Africa), and Severiano Ballesteros (Spain) twice.

The original links were laid out in 1886, and ten years later they moved the small distance to their present site. It was designated a "royal" course in 1926. The first championship at Lytham was the 1893 British Ladies championship.

Lytham is flat compared to some of the Scottish links, but the wind that blows in from the Fylde estuary makes it as tough as any of

its Scottish rivals. And it demands complete accuracy off the tee, as Gary Player confirmed by using a one iron as opposed to a wood when he won the Open in 1974. Any lapse in concentration is severely punished by the hidden dangers of Lytham's links. The closing two holes, while not the severest in championship golf, can pose problems if concentration goes at that crucial time. Jack Nicklaus will bear that out: he needed two par fours at those holes to capture his first Open in 1963. He took fives.

Large crowds flock around Lytham's 18th hole, a great Championship closing hole.

SCORECARD					
Hole	Yards	Par	Hole	Yards	Par
1	206	3	10	334	4
2	420	4	11	485	5
3	458	4	12	189	3
4	393	4	13	339	4
5	188	3	14	445	4
6	486	5	15	468	4
7	551	5	16	356	4
8	394	4	17	413	4
9	162	3	18	386	4
Out	3,258	35	In	3,415	36
TOTALS				6,673	71

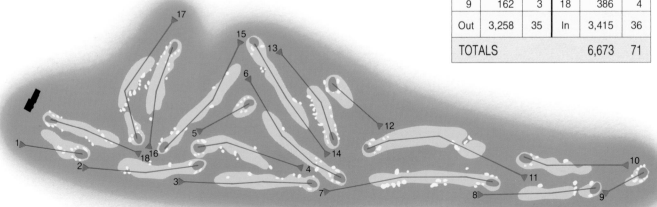

ROYAL ST. GEORGE'S

THE ST. GEORGE'S Club was founded in 1887, and seven years later it became the first English course to stage the British Open. Between then and 1949, it played host to the world's greatest tournament ten times. But the facilities and amenities at nearby Sandwich, in southeastern England, were becoming inadequate for the vast army of fans flocking to the Open in those post-war years, and it was removed from the Open roster until 1981. Four years later, Sandwich witnessed the first British success in "her" Open for 16 years when Sandy Lyle beat the world.

St. George's is a very undulating course and to have one leg three or four inches shorter than the other would be a great advantage. Large bunkers and the wind are additional hazards.

St. George's has witnessed some memorable moments, none finer than Tony Jacklin performing the first-ever televised hole-in-one in Britain during the 1967 Dunlop Masters at the short 16th. And it was at St. George's in 1922 that the flamboyant Walter Hagen became the first American-born winner of the British Open. That

was the start of a domination that has more or less lasted 70 years. In 1930, the great Bobby Jones led the American team to victory in the first Walker Cup match played in England, and four years later Britain's Henry Cotton set St. George's alight with blistering

rounds of 67 and 65 as he captured the first of his three Open titles.

The triangle of holes constituting the 13th, 14th, and 15th in the far corner of the course are where rounds are made or broken. Each of the three greens at those holes is surrounded by bunkers. But survive those three, and the homeward run is not too difficult.

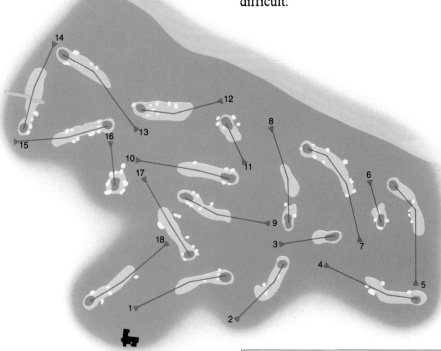

Royal St. George's Old Course

SCORECARD

Hole	Yards	Par	Hole	Yards	Par
1	445	4	10	399	4
2	376	4	11	216	3
3	214	3	12	362	4
4	470	4	13	443	4
5	422	4	14	508	5
6	156	3	15	467	4
7	529	5	16	165	3
8	415	4	17	425	4
9	387	4	18	458	4
Out	3,414	35	In	3,443	35
TOTALS				6,857	70

Many of the great English courses are ringed with expensive houses. St. George's is no exception.

SUNNINGDALE

SITUATED IN BERKSHIRE, the Sunningdale golf club, with its Old and New courses, provides some of the finest golf in southern England.

Founded in 1900, the Old course was laid out by Willie Park and the New course, designed by Harry Colt, was completed in 1922. A prestigious club, it has had two royal captains over the years, with Edward VIII filling that role when he was Prince of Wales, and George VI taking up the captaincy when he was the Duke of York.

While the Old course has been used for some major events, like the Dunlop Masters, over the years and as a qualifying venue for the British Open, it is a bit too small for major championships. However, the popular Sunningdale Foursomes have been held there since 1934. And since 1982, the European Open has been staged at Sunningdale eight times.

Gary Player won his first British professional tournament, the Dunlop Tournament, at Sunningdale in 1956, when he shot a course record 64. The record was lowered to 61 by Peter Butler during the 1967 Bowmaker Tournament.

Sunningdale is one of England's finest golf courses. However, because of its location, it is not an Open Championship venue.

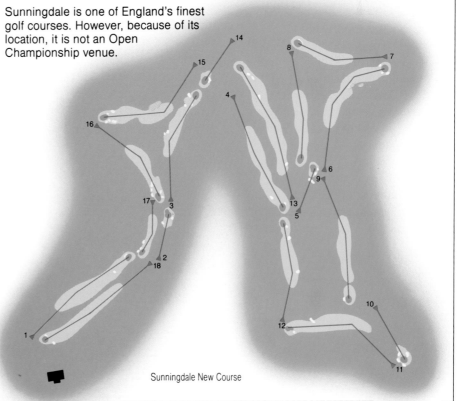

Sunningdale New Course

SCORECARD					
Hole	Yards	Par	Hole	Yards	Par
1	466	4	10	213	3
2	175	3	11	453	4
3	396	4	12	400	4
4	436	4	13	553	5
5	190	3	14	194	3
6	492	5	15	446	4
7	383	4	16	385	4
8	402	4	17	175	3
9	440	4	18	477	5
Out	3,380	35	In	3,296	35
TOTALS				6,676	70

WENTWORTH

SITUATED AT VIRGINIA Water, Surrey, Wentworth is one of England's best-known courses and has been used for major championships since its opening in 1924. It has not staged the British Open, though, because it is not a links course.

The East Course was the first to be opened, and it was followed by the West Course in the 1930s. But it was not until after the war that the latter became established as Wentworth's championship course. Because of its length, nearly 7,000 yards, it was nicknamed the "Burma Road." And its par-5 17th, with its dogleg left, is one of the game's great long holes - a view confirmed by Arnold Palmer.

The home of the World Matchplay Championship every year, Wentworth has also played host to all the great team competitions including the Ryder Cup and Canada Cup (now the World Cup). The forerunner of the Ryder Cup, a match between British and American professionals, was held at Wentworth in 1926. The Volvo PGA Championship, one of the top PGA European Tour events, is played at Wentworth each year and, because of its close location to London, it is a very popular course for Pro-Am and celebrity events. The course has undergone many changes in the last 20 years.

The clubhouse at Wentworth, Virginia Water, Surrey in southern England.

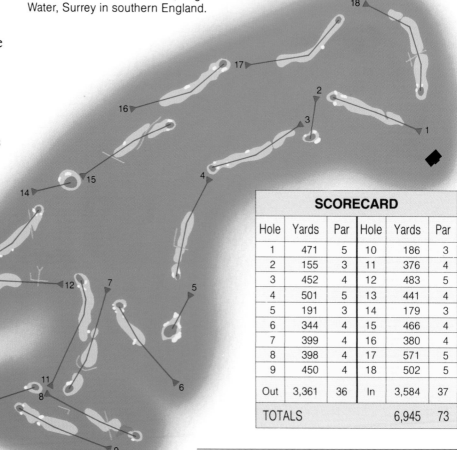

Wentworth West Course

SCORECARD

Hole	Yards	Par	Hole	Yards	Par
1	471	5	10	186	3
2	155	3	11	376	4
3	452	4	12	483	5
4	501	5	13	441	4
5	191	3	14	179	3
6	344	4	15	466	4
7	399	4	16	380	4
8	398	4	17	571	5
9	450	4	18	502	5
Out	3,361	36	In	3,584	37
TOTALS				6,945	73

Above Nick Faldo driving at one of Wentworth's tree-lined fairways. On this occasion it is also "spectator-lined."

Left A large gallery skirts the green at Wentworth's 18th during the 1989 PGA Championship won by Nick Faldo.

CHANTILLY

The impressive Chantilly clubhouse.

NOT ONLY IS Chantilly one of the oldest golf courses in France, it is also one of the finest.

Dating from 1908, it has staged the French Open many times, the first in 1913 when George Duncan took the title.

Situated 25 miles (40km) north of Paris, it is a typical shrubland course set amid woodland. Its 6,500 meters (approximately 7,040 yards) offer one of the most testing of challenges in Europe.

The present-day championship course was designed by Tom Simpson in the 1920s, but much of his good work was ruined by World War II bombs. When it was rebuilt, much of his original design was retained. Three of the four par-3s are over 190 meters (208 yards) long, which make its par-71 one of the toughest to achieve.

Set in woodland, it has been designed to give ample room to play golf without having to worry constantly about the trees. But the enclosure created by the trees gives an atmosphere of isolation, and there are no distractions.

Britain's Peter Oosterhuis won the French Open at Chantilly in 1974. The next time Chantilly hosted the championship in 1988, another Briton, Nick Faldo, captured the title. And 12 months later at the same venue he made it back-to-back victories.

SCORECARD					
Hole	Meters	Par	Hole	Meters	Par
1	418	4	10	434	4
2	362	4	11	389	4
3	158	3	12	368	4
4	358	4	13	418	4
5	397	4	14	199	3
6	198	3	15	381	4
7	401	4	16	193	3
8	527	5	17	392	4
9	459	5	18	545	5
Out	3,278	36	In	3,319	35
TOTALS				6,597	71

St. Nom-la-Breteche

THE ST. NOM-LA-BRETECHE is situated 15 miles from Paris close to Versailles. The original course was laid out by the British designer Fred Hawtree.

It has three times been used for the French Open, the first being in 1965 when Ramon Sota of Spain shot a course record 62. When it was last held there in 1982, it was won by Sota's nephew, Severiano Ballesteros.

The Versailles course has played host to the end-of-season Lancôme Trophy since it was first held in 1970.

There are two other courses at St. Nom-la-Breteche, the Red and Blue.

SCORECARD

Hole	Meters	Par	Hole	Meters	Par
1	333	4	10	382	4
2	381	4	11	341	4
3	173	3	12	498	5
4	363	4	13	196	3
5	444	5	14	325	4
6	400	4	15	362	4
7	465	5	16	175	3
8	386	4	17	465	5
9	191	3	18	332	4
Out	3,136	36	In	3,076	36
TOTALS				6,212	72

Players practice their putting before the 1989 Lancôme Trophy at St. Nom-la-Breteche.

Did You Know?

An estimated 300 million golf balls are sold worldwide each year.

ROYAL COUNTY DOWN

THE SETTING OF the Royal County Down course, some 30 miles south of Belfast, Northern Ireland, makes it one of Ireland's truly picturesque courses. The backdrop of the Mountains of Mourne and the shores of Dundrum Bay make it one of the great seaside courses.

The club was formed in 1889, and the committee recruited the services of Tom Morris to lay out the course at a cost of "not more than £4." It doesn't seem much, but Tom managed it, thanks largely to the wonderful natural resources the area offered.

It received royal patronage in 1908 when it stood as one of the finest courses in the British Isles.

John Ball won the first national championship to be played at County Down in 1893, and five years later the first professional tournament was won by Harry Vardon, who was a great lover of the Ulster course. Vardon loved it so much that day that he beat his great rival J. H. Taylor 12 and 11.

While the course would do justice to a major championship

like the British Open, the lack of nearby qualifying courses and accommodation means it has been overlooked. But who knows? Royal County Down could become the second Irish course to stage the Open Championship.

Right Royal County Down on a gray and murky day with the backdrop of the Mountains of Mourne.

SCORECARD

Hole	Yards	Par	Hole	Yards	Par
1	506	5	10	200	3
2	424	4	11	440	4
3	473	4	12	501	5
4	217	3	13	445	4
5	440	4	14	213	3
6	396	4	15	445	4
7	145	3	16	265	4
8	427	4	17	400	4
9	486	5	18	545	5
Out	3,514	36	In	3,454	36
TOTALS				6,968	72

ROYAL PORTRUSH

ROYAL PORTRUSH HOLDS a special place in British Open history because it is the only Irish course to play host to the world's greatest tournament. That was back in 1951 when Britain's Max Faulkner captured the title.

Founded in 1888, Portrush, with its three courses, is steeped in history and tradition. The best known of the courses is the championship Dunluce course. Originally known as the Country Club, Portrush was granted Royal patronage by the Duke of York in 1892, and in 1895 it became the Royal Portrush Golf Club with the Prince of Wales (later King Edward VII) as patron.

Originally a nine-hole course, a second nine were added within a year. Changes over the years have resulted in many holes moving outward toward the sand dunes, making it as severe a test as any links course in the British Isles.

The fairways on the Dunluce course are all narrow and, with the exception of the first and last holes, are doglegged. The 11th, because of its location, can be anything from a medium iron to a full-blooded wood off the tee, depending upon which way the wind is blowing.

Left A view across the Portrush course with the town in the background.

SCORECARD					
Hole	Yards	Par	Hole	Yards	Par
1	389	4	10	480	5
2	497	5	11	166	3
3	159	3	12	395	4
4	455	4	13	371	4
5	384	4	14	213	3
6	193	3	15	366	4
7	432	4	16	432	4
8	376	4	17	517	5
9	476	5	18	481	5
Out	3,361	36	In	3,421	37
TOTALS				6,782	73

Left Action at Royal Portrush's 11th. It remains the only Irish course to host the British Open.

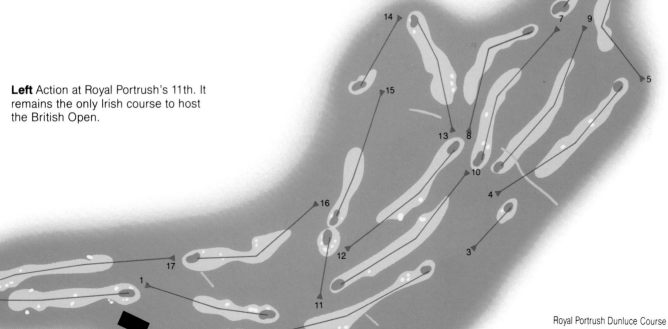

Royal Portrush Dunluce Course

PENINA

SITUATED IN THE Algarve, that popular golfing area of southern Portugal, Penina was designed on bare flat fields by one of Britain's best-loved golfers, Henry Cotton, in 1964.

More than a quarter of a million trees and shrubs transformed the bare land into a beautiful golf course. Cotton set up his home at Penina and spent much of his later life there.

Cotton designed the course as only a champion could. It is long, and each shot must be planned in advance. Haste is a foolhardy gamble at Penina. Time and pre-planning are two important essentials when playing the 6,439-meter (7,042-yard) course.

Henry Cotton used the course for his golf school, and the PGA Tour has continued the tradition by taking young hopefuls to that area of Portugal each year for a coaching program. Cotton is no longer with us, but his dream certainly is.

SCORECARD

Hole	Meters	Par	Hole	Meters	Par
1	411	4	10	500	5
2	401	4	11	491	5
3	301	4	12	397	4
4	375	4	13	208	3
5	463	5	14	394	4
6	186	3	15	318	4
7	299	4	16	210	3
8	180	3	17	450	5
9	405	4	18	450	5
Out	3,021	35	In	3,418	38
TOTALS				6,439	73

Left The Penina Hotel dominates the background at Portugal's best known course.

Below The great climate and sun help make the Penina setting even more beautiful.

CARNOUSTIE

WHEN USED FOR the British Open in 1968, Carnoustie's course, at 7,252 yards, became the longest ever in Open history. It was first used for the Championship in 1931, when Tommy Armour of the United States was the winner. It has been used five times in all, the last being in 1975 when Tom Watson beat the luckless Australian Jack Newton to win his first title.

The course held no fear for Ben Hogan, who won three of the four Majors in 1953 including the Open. Even the monster par-five 6th didn't bother him, and he twice birdied the hole on the last day in winning the title.

Built on public ground at Angus, the club was founded in 1842. Many natural hazards make the course difficult, and the closing three holes are probably the toughest in championship golf in Britain. The 235-yard par-3 16th requires the best of tee shots, and the last two, the Island and Home holes, each require the Barry Burn to be negotiated. Jockie's Burn zigzags its way across the course and adds to the problems at four of the first six holes.

Carnoustie's 7,252 yards make it the longest course ever used for the British Open, staged there in 1968.

SCORECARD

Hole	Yards	Par	Hole	Yards	Par
1	416	4	10	452	4
2	460	4	11	358	4
3	347	4	12	475	5
4	434	4	13	168	3
5	393	4	14	488	5
6	575	5	15	461	4
7	397	4	16	235	3
8	183	3	17	455	4
9	474	4	18	486	4
Out	3,679	36	In	3,593	36
TOTALS				7,252	72

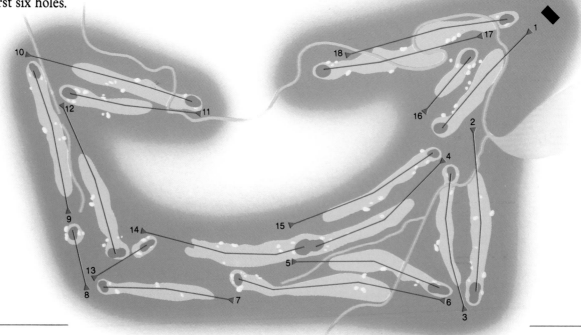

GLENEAGLES

BECAUSE IT IS not a links course, Gleneagles has never staged the British Open. Nevertheless, it is one of the most beautiful courses in Britain, steeped in tradition.

Two of the world's most famous golfers designed the three championship courses at The Gleneagles Hotel in Scotland. James Braid, five times winner of the Open championship, designed the King's and Queen's at the beginning of the century, and now the great Jack Nicklaus has designed the Monarch's.

The original design of the King's and Queen's represents some of the finest examples of "classical" golf course design. The King's is outward-looking and the Queen's predominantly inward. The Monarch's, best described as a "modern classic," is a combination of both.

Home of the Bell's Scottish Open, the King's Course has a traditional Scottish layout described as "straight out and straight in." The fairways are generous in width and the greens large, approximately 600 square meters (720 square yards). The magnificent course offers the golfer a real challenge, especially on the last few holes, where the 17th runs into the wind after playing the previous four holes downwind. In return it provides breathtaking vistas of the hillsides, moorland, and glens among which the hotel is set.

The beautiful Queen's is generally considered easier than the King's. Essentially it requires shorter second shots to the greens, and the good bunkering provides a demanding test for the golfer. The course typifies the "Gleneagles golfing experience" with a design which tests the golfer, combined with stunning scenery.

People come to Gleneagles to stay at the famous Gleneagles Hotel, as well as to play golf; both are spectacular.

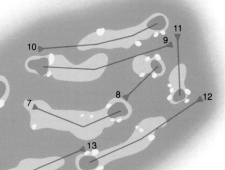

Gleneagles King's Course

SCORECARD					
Hole	Yards	Par	Hole	Yards	Par
1	362	4	10	447	4
2	405	4	11	230	3
3	374	4	12	395	4
4	466	4	13	448	4
5	161	3	14	260	4
6	476	5	15	459	4
7	439	4	16	135	3
8	158	3	17	377	4
9	354	4	18	525	5
Out	3,195	35	In	3,276	35
TOTALS				6,471	70

MUIRFIELD

AFTER LEAVING THEIR Musselburgh home, the Honourable Company of Edinburgh Golfers took up their new home at Muirfield in 1892.

Situated on the shores of the Firth of Forth, the famous course has played host to the British Open 14 times, with the 1992 Championship being held there to mark the 100th anniversary of Muirfield's first Open, which was won by Harold Hilton, an Englishman.

Muirfield's near-7,000 yard course is a very testing one and is a "true" championship course. The world's leading professionals have nothing but the utmost respect for it.

One of the big problems at Muirfield, like all links courses, is the wind. Few holes run in the

Below One of Muirfield's bunkers in the foreground with the clubhouse in the background.

Right Muirfield's 13th green.

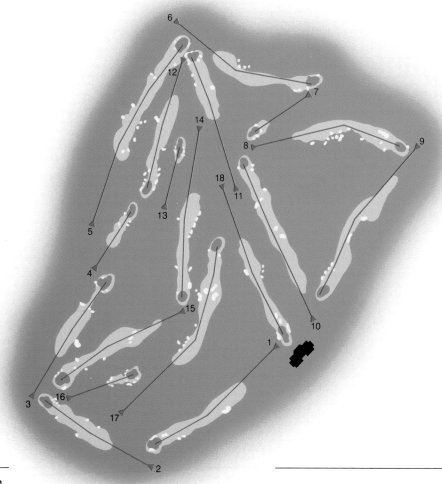

SCORECARD					
Hole	Yards	Par	Hole	Yards	Par
1	447	4	10	475	4
2	351	4	11	385	4
3	379	4	12	381	4
4	180	3	13	159	3
5	559	5	14	449	4
6	469	4	15	417	4
7	185	3	16	188	3
8	444	4	17	550	5
9	504	5	18	448	4
Out	3,518	36	In	3,452	35
TOTALS				6,970	71

same direction, so it is difficult to keep track of the wind. The narrow fairways and the relatively small greens add further to Muirfield's severity. And the two closing holes are among the sternest in championship golf, demanding the most accurate of tee shots.

But the best names in golf have beaten both wind and course to capture the Open at Muirfield. There was Henry Cotton's brilliant display of driving in 1948, Gary Player in 1959 when he won his first Open, and Jack Nicklaus beating the severe rough to take his first title in 1966. Nicklaus later named his own course in Ohio after the famous Scottish links. And for sheer magic there was Lee Trevino's chip at the 71st hole which went into the cup and destroyed Tony Jacklin's chances of a second British Open title in 1972. They were all memorable Open occasions at Muirfield.

The course has also staged other leading tournaments, including all the top amateur events, and in 1973 the Ryder Cup was played in Scotland for the first and only time at Muirfield's famous links.

Muirfield has a big advantage over some other championship courses; it is a great spectator course offering many fine vantage points. Consequently it remains very much part of the British Open roster.

PRESTWICK

AYRSHIRE'S PRESTWICK COURSE is no longer the great championship course it was. But its place in British Open history should never be forgotten.

The first major professional championship in the world, the British Open, was played over Prestwick's 12-hole links in 1860, and the famous Scottish course staged every championship up to 1872, thereafter sharing it with Musselburgh and St. Andrews.

Golf had been played at Prestwick for many years before the course was laid out on publicly owned land in 1851. The splendid, sea-washed turf made it a very attractive course to play on in those days, and the small greens set among undulating hollows made it a severe test for the best of golfers like Allan Robertson.

It was after Robertson's death that the Prestwick club organized the first Open championship to find his successor as "champion golfer of the four Kingdoms."

Three rounds of Prestwick's 12 holes made up the first Open, won by Willie Park of Musselburgh. It became an 18-hole course in 1883, and the first Amateur Championship was held at Prestwick in 1888. Over the following years, it became established as one of the great championship courses.

However, in the years after World War I, and with the new breed of American professional making the trip across the Atlantic for the Open each year, it was no longer the severe test it used to be, and the two short closing holes were far too easy for such an event. Furthermore, its location made it a difficult course for spectators to reach, and in 1925 Prestwick

The famous Cardinal Bunker which makes Prestwick's par-5 third hole even more testing.

staged its last British Open. However, the Amateur Championship continued to be played at Prestwick until the 1950s. It remained very much a male stronghold and did not even have ladies' tees until they were installed for the 1978 Scottish

Ladies' Championship.

Despite no longer being a major championship course, Prestwick remains a crucial stopping-off point for golfers who make annual trips to the famous Scottish courses, as they have not forgotten its place in golfing history.

SCORECARD					
Hole	Yards	Par	Hole	Yards	Par
1	346	4	10	454	4
2	167	3	11	195	3
3	482	5	12	513	5
4	382	4	13	460	4
5	206	3	14	362	4
6	362	4	15	347	4
7	430	4	16	288	4
8	431	4	17	391	4
9	444	4	18	284	4
Out	3,250	35	In	3,294	36
TOTALS				6,544	71

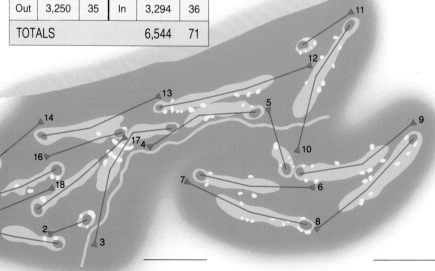

ROYAL DORNOCH

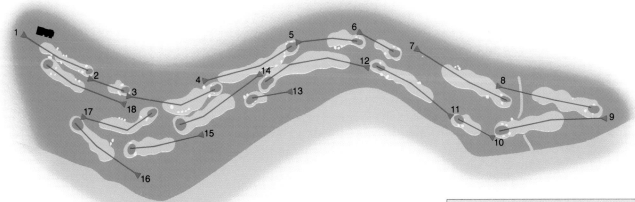

SCORECARD					
Hole	Yards	Par	Hole	Yards	Par
1	332	4	10	150	3
2	182	3	11	445	4
3	413	4	12	516	5
4	418	4	13	168	3
5	357	4	14	445	4
6	164	3	15	323	4
7	463	4	16	400	4
8	437	4	17	410	4
9	497	5	18	461	4
Out	3,263	35	In	3,318	35
TOTALS				6,581	70

ROYAL DORNOCH IS the northernmost first-class golf course in Britain. Situated on the southeastern coast of Sutherland, there are two courses, with the Old course the most famous.

Because of the Gulf Stream, golf is played all year round without the problems that the winter months bring to other British courses. Had it been located in a more accessible part of Scotland, it would almost certainly have served as an Open venue, because it is a true links course and those who have played it will testify to its acceptability as a championship venue.

Golf was played at Dornoch in the early 17th century, although the Dornoch Golf Club was not founded until 1877. A few years later, Tom Morris, Sr., was commissioned to lay out a nine-hole course.

It soon became an 18-hole course, and under the direction of John Sutherland, secretary of the club for 50 years, it was elevated to a championship-rated course in 1904. In the pre-war years, all the leading professionals of the day made a point of playing exhibition and money matches at Dornoch - Vardon described the 14th as the finest natural golf hole he had ever played.

Small, well-guarded greens make Dornoch a demanding course, and the variable wind offered by its location makes it as difficult as any links course.

The spectacular setting of Britain's northernmost first-class golf course; Royal Dornoch.

ROYAL TROON

UNDULATING FAIRWAYS AND severe rough, plus its location, make Troon one of the most testing of British championship courses.

Situated north of Ayr on the west coast of Scotland, six of Troon's holes run alongside the Firth of Clyde, where wind poses the biggest problem. Gales are said to be so severe at times that fish have been washed up on the greens!

The club was founded in 1878 and was first added to the list of British Open courses in 1923 when Arthur Havers won. The second Open here was not until after the war, when South African Bobby Locke captured the title. It has been used four more times, the last in 1989 when American Mark Calcavecchia was the surprise winner after a playoff.

Arnold Palmer lowered the 72-hole British Open record to 276 at Troon when winning his second successive title in 1962, and 11 years later Tom Weiskopf equaled the record.

The longest hole in Open history was Troon's 577-yard 6th,

and the shortest was also at Troon – the notorious Postage Stamp hole (8th) measured 126 yards in 1973. It was at the Postage Stamp that 71-year-old Gene Sarazen holed-in-one in front of the television cameras during that year. But German amateur Herman Tissies took 15 strokes at the Postage Stamp during the 1950 Open.

Troon was granted royal status in its centenary year, 1978.

Below Tom Kite playing to one of Britain's best-known holes, Troon's 8th, the "Postage Stamp."

Bottom left Fans enthralled by the action during the 1989 Open at Troon which provided a surprise winner, Mark Calcavecchia of the United States.

SCORECARD

Hole	Yards	Par	Hole	Yards	Par
1	364	4	10	438	4
2	391	4	11	481	5
3	379	4	12	431	4
4	557	5	13	465	4
5	210	3	14	179	3
6	577	5	15	457	4
7	402	4	16	542	5
8	126	3	17	223	3
9	423	4	18	452	4
Out	3,429	36	In	3,668	36
TOTALS				7,097	72

A view of the "Postage Stamp" from tee to pin. It was at this hole in 1973 that 71-year-old Gene Sarazen holed-in-one during the Open.

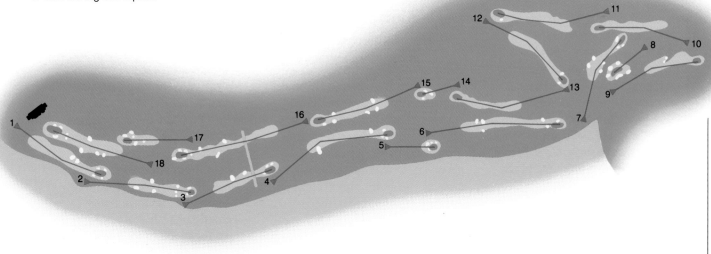

St. Andrews

ST. ANDREWS IS regarded as the "home" of golf. And why not? Golf has been played in the Burgh since the 16th century, and probably earlier.

The first record of golf at St. Andrews was in 1552, but it is safe to assume it was played there some years earlier and possibly in 1457 when King James II banned the playing of golf because it interfered with archery practice.

The Society of St. Andrews Golfers was formed at a meeting on May 12, 1754. The site of the original clubhouse is unknown, but it is known that the members used to fill themselves with food and drink at Baillie Glass's before moving on to the Union Parlour. The present clubhouse was erected in 1854, one hundred years after the formation of the Society. Twenty years earlier, in 1834, the club had changed its name to the Royal and Ancient Golf Club (R & A) after King William IV agreed to become the club's first patron. Captaincy of the R & A remains

one of the game's greatest honors.

The R & A gained in popularity toward the end of the 19th century, and after more and more clubs turned to it for clarification on rules of the game, it officially became the governing authority on the rules in 1897.

The original St. Andrews course, alongside St. Andrews Bay, was a 22-hole course, but had only 12 huge greens. Players started alongside the home hole (22nd) and played 11 holes out before turning and playing the same holes again, but in the opposite direction.

The first four holes were later reduced to two, which cut down the number of greens to ten and the holes to 18. However, golf became dangerous with sets of players hitting balls in opposite directions. It was therefore necessary to widen the fairways and cut two holes into each green. And the double-holed greens remain a feature of the Old Course. Today there are eleven

greens, seven of them double greens.

A second course, the New Course, was added in 1894. The Jubilee course was completed in 1897 and in 1912 the Eden Course, needed to meet the increased demands, was completed.

It was anticipated in the early days that golf would be free to all at St. Andrews, but such was the demand that green fees were eventually charged for the first time in 1913.

The Old Course is the one that is used for all major championships, and it staged the first of its record-equaling 24 British Opens in 1873. In the early days of championship golf, many champions came from St. Andrews. Notably there were

Far left The St. Andrews clubhouse.

Left The 17th at St. Andrews, the "Road Hole."

Below Mark James playing to the "Road Hole."

SCORECARD					
Hole	Yards	Par	Hole	Yards	Par
1	370	4	10	342	4
2	411	4	11	172	3
3	371	4	12	316	4
4	463	4	13	425	4
5	564	5	14	567	5
6	416	4	15	413	4
7	372	4	16	382	4
8	178	3	17	461	4
9	356	4	18	354	4
Out	3,501	36	In	3,432	36
TOTALS				6,933	72

Andrew Strath and Old and Young Tom Morris.

Apart from its double greens, a major feature of St. Andrews is the many huge bunkers, including the Hell bunker, which awaits any wayward shot on the 14th. And many great golfers have flirted with trouble in the Hell bunker over the years.

The Road Hole, the 17th, is a 461-yard par-4, but can be one of the most difficult in world golf. Many great rounds have fallen apart at this one hole. And for sheer excitement, the walk up the 18th fairway to the last green with the magnificent clubhouse in front of you is one of the great moments in golf.

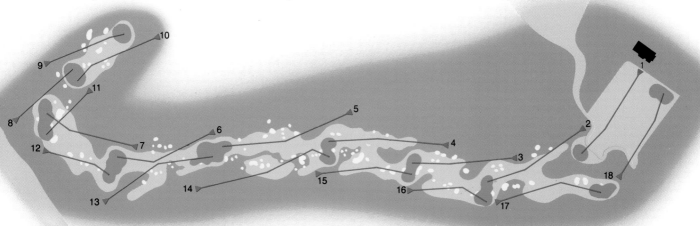

TURNBERRY

WITH THE BEAUTIFUL backdrop of the Ailsa Craig and Isle of Arran, Turnberry has one of the finest settings of all championship courses in Britain.

Golf was played at Turnberry in the last century when the Marquis of Ailsa had a private course on his Culzean estate. But it was not until 1903 that the Turnberry Hotel Golf Club was founded. The second course was laid out between the world wars, and the two courses were named the Ailsa and Arran courses. The Ailsa is the championship course used today.

Perhaps strangely, Turnberry was not used for its first British Open until 1977, when Tom Watson and Jack Nicklaus engaged in a great battle which saw British Open records tumble.

Because of its geographic location, Turnberry's links were requisitioned during both wars, and during World War II, it was extensively damaged when its links were used as runways by the RAF. But thanks to the efforts of Frank Hole, and the skills of course architect Mackenzie Ross, Turnberry was opened again in 1951.

Ross's "new" courses soon gained rave reviews and in the early 1950s Turnberry was used for the Scottish National Championships. When the *News of the World* Matchplay Championship and Walker Cup were held there, it was hailed as a great championship course and eventually joined the list of British Open courses.

The Turnberry Hotel is popular with tourists, particularly the Japanese, and in 1987 the 133-room hotel and two courses passed into Japanese hands for $24 million.

Above Turnberry offers not only the finest golf, but also the best in hotels.

Above right The lighthouse is one of Turnberry's many natural features.

Right Action from the 1989 Seniors Championship at Turnberry which was won by New Zealander Bob Charles.

SCORECARD					
Hole	Yards	Par	Hole	Yards	Par
1	350	4	10	452	4
2	428	4	11	177	3
3	462	4	12	448	4
4	167	3	13	411	4
5	441	4	14	440	4
6	222	3	15	209	3
7	528	5	16	409	4
8	427	4	17	500	5
9	455	4	18	431	4
Out	3,480	35	In	3,477	35
TOTALS				6,957	70

Turnberry Ailsa Course

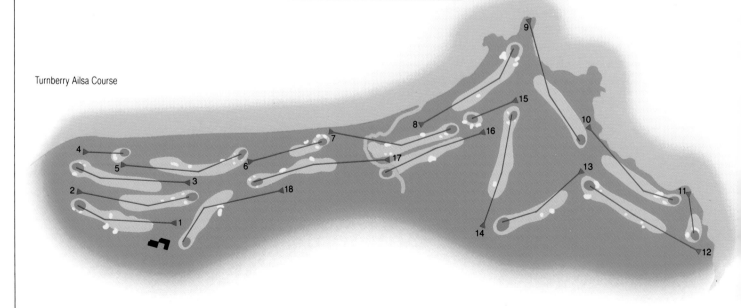

VALDERRAMA

SITUATED ON SPAIN'S Costa del Sol, Valderrama is rapidly gaining a reputation as "Europe's Augusta."

Set among beautiful cork trees at Sotogrande, the course was originally laid out in 1964 by Robert Trent Jones, and two years later it hosted the Spanish Open. That championship was won by Argentinian Roberto de Vicenzo, who shot a second round 66, which included a three-putt from a mere five yards on the last green.

Formerly known as Los Aves, the course was acquired by a Spanish industrialist and a consortium of seven friends in 1985 who wanted to turn it into an exclusive private club, but at the same time make it a challenging championship course. The latter was achieved when Jones was again called in to make the necessary changes. Its 6,353 meters (6,951 yards) par 71, make Valderrama one of the great championship courses on the European Tour, and the back nine holes rank among the toughest on the Tour.

Situated close to the Mediterranean, Valderrama offers not only a stiff challenge to any golfer, but also some wonderful panoramic views which can often distract the player from the job in hand . . . trying to conquer the course!

Valderrama has hosted the Volvo Masters since its inauguration in 1988 when Britain's Nick Faldo carried off the title.

Right José-Maria Olazabal plays the 15th hole in the 1989 Volvo Masters.

Below Beautiful and lush, Valderrama is an enchanting course.

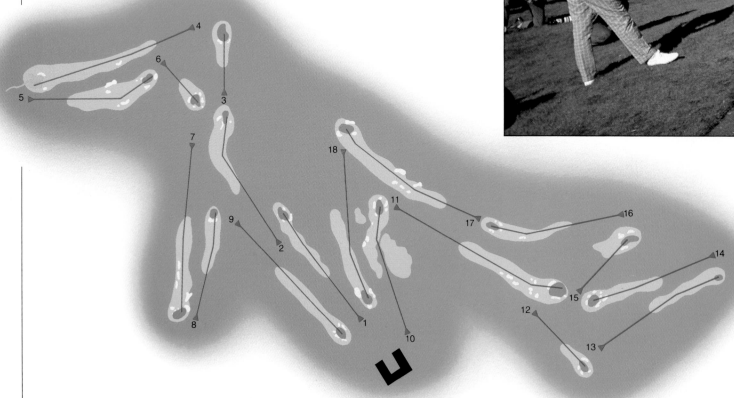

SCORECARD					
Hole	Meters	Par	Hole	Meters	Par
1	354	4	10	369	4
2	375	4	11	504	5
3	156	3	12	200	3
4	515	5	13	367	4
5	344	4	14	337	4
6	150	3	15	207	3
7	420	4	16	385	4
8	319	4	17	519	5
9	415	4	18	417	4
Out	3,048	35	In	3,305	36
TOTALS				6,353	71

CRANS-SUR-SIERRE

THE HOME OF the Swiss Open since 1939, the Crans-sur-Sierre Golf Club is situated 5,000 feet above the Rhône Valley and is overlooked by the Matterhorn. Its setting is spectacular.

The first Crans course was laid out by Sir Arnold Lunn, an international skiing pioneer, in 1905. He had already built the Palace Hotel, but the tourists never came as expected and the course closed during World War I. Attempts to revive golf in the area were mooted in 1923, and in 1927 the current courses were opened. The rarified altitude helps the ball off the tee.

During the 1978 Open, José-Maria Olazabal of Spain established a European record of 27 strokes for nine holes, and during the 1971 Open Italy's Baldovino Dassu established a European record of 60 for 18 holes which still stands today.

The course is covered with snow in the winter months, but when the snow clears, it always comes back to its former glory. It is the largest club in Switzerland.

SCORECARD					
Hole	Meters	Par	Hole	Meters	Par
1	490	5	10	370	4
2	395	4	11	190	3
3	165	3	12	355	4
4	460	4	13	185	3
5	315	4	14	520	5
6	295	4	15	475	5
7	275	4	16	290	4
8	160	3	17	315	4
9	565	5	18	345	4
Out	3,120	36	In	3,045	36
TOTALS				6,165	72

The Crans-sur-Sierre course in the Rhône Valley is one of the most picturesque in Europe. Its setting in the shadow of the Matterhorn makes its location magnificent.

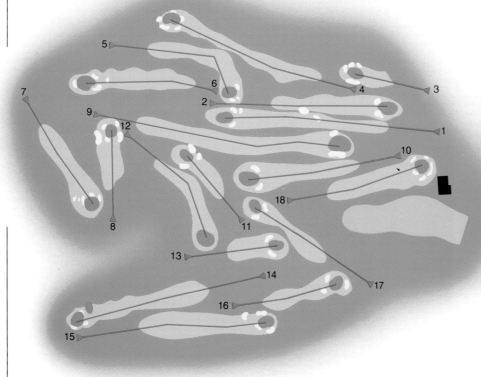

AUGUSTA

THE AUGUSTA NATIONAL course at Augusta, Georgia, is, without doubt, one of *the* great golf courses of the world. For sheer beauty it has no rival.

The Augusta course, and the Masters, which has been played here since its launch in 1934, were the brainchild of native Georgian Bobby Jones, who became one of the world's top golfers before his early retirement in 1930, and of his great friend Clifford Roberts.

They recruited the services of top golf-course designer Alister Mackenzie, and in 1931 the dream of the Augusta National came to fruition. Jones decided to call it the Augusta *National* because the intention was to attract people from all over the U.S. to his beautiful new course.

Each hole is named after the tree, shrub, or plant that lines the fairway, and the names of the 18 holes are reminders of the days when the 385-acre site was a nursery. The names of the holes are as follows:

1	Tea Olive	10	Camellia
2	Pink Dogwood	11	White Dogwood
3	Flowering Peach	12	Golden Bell
4	Crabapple	13	Azalea
5	Magnolia	14	Chinese Fir
6	Juniper	15	Firethorn
7	Pampas	16	Redbud
8	Yellow Jasmine	17	Nandina
9	Carolina Cherry	18	Holly

The tall pine trees, often creating giant shadows across the course, are a major feature of Augusta. And the lakes offer not only beauty but a challenge to the very best of golfers. The lake in front of the 16th green has been the end of many a fine round.

Each hole must be pre-calculated, and playing on the putting surfaces requires the very best eye to read the greens - they have numerous twists, turns, and rolls, and are among the fastest in the world. How many times have you seen a putt look like it's going into the hole at Augusta, then roll away by feet, not inches?

Jones played each hole countless times before he decided on the placements of the greens and other features, and he knew when it was finished that only the best would conquer Augusta. One man to do so is Jack Nicklaus, who has won the coveted Masters green jacket six times.

The course has altered only slightly since Jones's original idea, although the front nine and back nine have now swapped places.

The turning point in so many rounds at Augusta comes at the Amen Corner, which is a name given to the 11th, 12th, and 13th holes. They run alongside Rae's Creek, and water awaits any shots off course.

Augusta is the only course to stage a Major every year, and it has seen some memorable moments since the inauguration of the Masters in 1934. It was only one year old when Gene Sarazen had a remarkable double eagle at the par-5 15th, still a much-talked-about golf shot down Georgia way. And in 1987, Larry Mize's chip at the second extra playoff hole, the 11th, from the rough 30 yards from the hole, beat Greg Norman and captured him his first Major.

The home of the Masters has seen some great moments, as befits the most beautiful golf course in the world.

Above left The Augusta clubhouse.

Left The 10th, just one of Augusta's many spectacular holes.

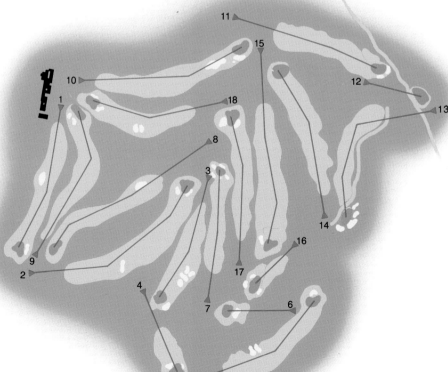

One of the features at Augusta is the water adjacent to many greens; the 16th is one such hole.

SCORECARD					
Hole	Yards	Par	Hole	Yards	Par
1	400	4	10	485	4
2	555	5	11	455	4
3	360	4	12	155	3
4	205	3	13	465	5
5	435	4	14	405	4
6	180	3	15	500	5
7	360	4	16	170	3
8	535	5	17	400	4
9	435	4	18	405	4
Out	3,465	36	In	3,440	36
TOTALS				6,905	72

BALTUSROL

ONE OF THE oldest golf clubs in the United States, Baltusrol is situated in Springfield, New Jersey. It was opened in 1895 and is named after a local farmer, Baltus Roll, who was murdered in 1825.

The course was laid out by Louis Keller, the owner and publisher of the *New York Social Register.* He owned the land at the foot of Baltusrol Mountain close to the New York state line.

It has played host to most leading American tournaments since it staged the US Ladies' Championship in 1901 and has hosted the US Open on six occasions. The first time was in 1903 when Willie Anderson won the first of his three consecutive titles. Appropriately, the Scottish-born Anderson was Baltusrol's first professional.

Baltusrol has not staged the Open since 1980, when Jack Nicklaus shattered US Open records for the lowest 18, 36, 54,

and 72 holes in winning his fourth, and last, title. The PGA Championship has never been played at Baltusrol.

The original course was plowed up in 1920 to make way for two new courses, the Upper and Lower, which were designed under the supervision of architect A. W. Tillinghast and opened in 1921. Both have staged the Open, the Upper in 1936.

The 17th hole on the Lower course is a 630-yard par-5 and is the longest hole ever to be played in the Open. It is one of the great championship holes.

No course has staged the US Open more times than Baltusrol's six occasions which, uniquely, have been over three different courses.

Right Baltusrol is one of the oldest golf clubs in the United States and, like many others, offers beauty as well as challenging golf.

Below right The tree-lined Lower Course at Baltusrol.

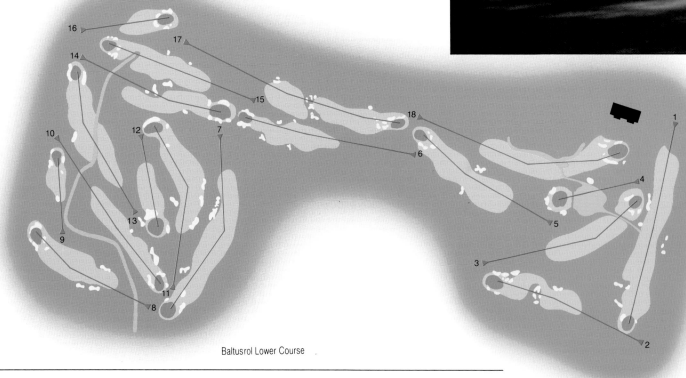

Baltusrol Lower Course

SCORECARD

Hole	Yards	Par	Hole	Yards	Par
1	478	5	10	454	4
2	381	4	11	428	4
3	443	4	12	193	3
4	194	3	13	393	4
5	393	4	14	409	4
6	470	4	15	430	4
7	505	5	16	216	3
8	374	4	17	630	5
9	205	3	18	542	5
Out	3,443	36	In	3,695	36
TOTALS				7,138	72

CYPRESS POINT

SITUATED ON THE Monterey peninsula in California, Cypress Point is 6,536 yards, not a long course but nevertheless a demanding one. Because of its length, it has never been used to stage a major championship.

The course offers great variety to the golfer, and its beauty attracts an army of photographers each year. Its 16th hole, like Pebble Beach's 7th, is a definite must for the camera buff.

The hole requires a carry of anything up to 200 yards across the Pacific, onto a green situated on a peninsula high above the ocean, which makes it not only a beautiful hole, but a potential disaster. Because of the severity of the 16th, many have described Cypress Point as "the best 17-hole golf course in the world"!

It is the 1921 US Women's Amateur Champion Marion Hollins who must take the credit for Cypress Point. She fell in love with California on visiting the area and decided to create a golf course. She raised the cash from local business people and sought the help of course designer Seth Raynor. But Raynor died suddenly before work on the course was started. Hollins turned to the top designer Alister Mackenzie, and in 1928 Cypress Point was opened to the public.

Mackenzie fully utilized the natural surroundings set in the shadow of the Santa Lucia Mountains and could have made the course even more spectacular than it is, but he resisted the temptation to create a golf course that was simply beautiful. He wanted to create a demanding test, and did so with great success. To compensate for the course's lack of length, he created deceptive greens with many hard-to-read contours.

Left A view of the 15th at Cypress Point with the backdrop of the Pacific Ocean lashing against the rocks.

Right There's no room for error at Cypress Point's 16th.

SCORECARD					
Hole	Yards	Par	Hole	Yards	Par
1	421	4	10	480	5
2	548	5	11	437	4
3	162	3	12	404	4
4	384	4	13	365	4
5	493	5	14	388	4
6	518	5	15	143	3
7	168	3	16	231	3
8	363	4	17	393	4
9	292	4	18	346	4
Out	3,349	37	In	3,187	35
TOTALS				6,536	72

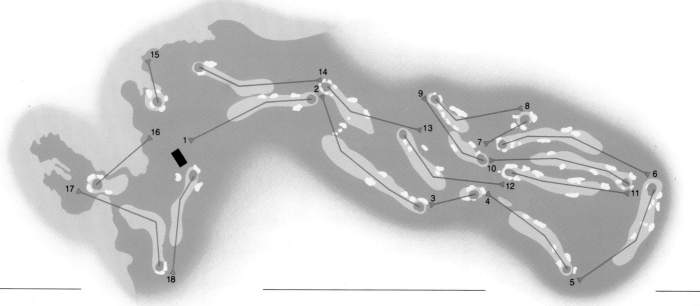

INVERNESS

ANOTHER OF AMERICA'S "older generation" golf courses, the Inverness Club in Toledo, Ohio, was opened in 1903. Its name, came from the Scottish Highland club of the same name, but, before naming it, members wrote to its Scottish counterpart seeking permission, which was readily granted. Since then, a long relationship has existed between the two clubs.

The original club was made up of two nine-hole courses, but in 1919 the Scottish designer Donald Ross merged the two into one 18-holer. A year later, the course was considered good enough to stage the US Open, and it was won by Ted Ray, the last English winner before Tony Jacklin 50 years later. Ray cut the corner of the dogleg 7th on each of his four rounds and picked up valuable birdies. It was a memorable Open because it was the championship debut for Bobby Jones, Tommy Armour, Gene Sarazen, Leo Diegel, and Bill Mehlhorn.

Billy Burke won the Open when it was next played at Inverness in 1931. It was the longest championship ever, requiring a 72-hole playoff. Mayer won over the

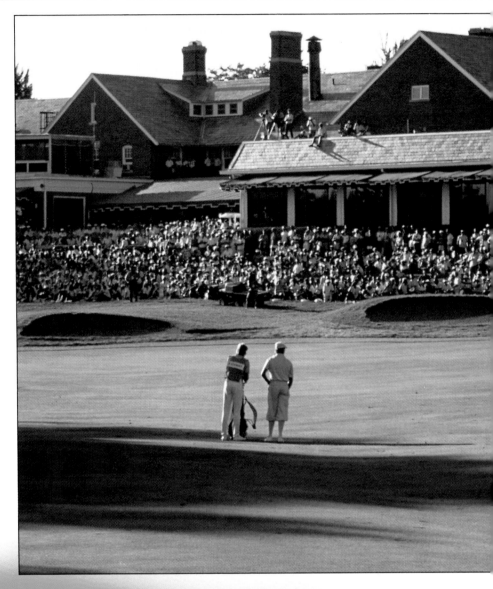

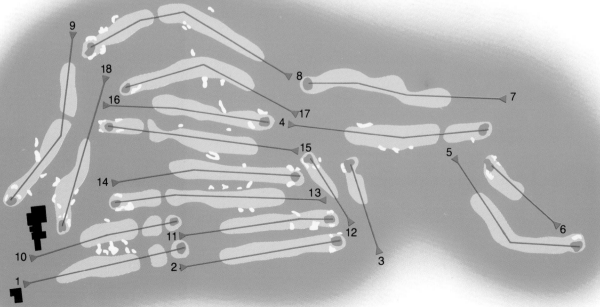

revised course in 1957, and in 1979 Hale Irwin captured his second title despite a final round 75.

Trees, normally a major feature of American courses, are in short supply at Inverness, but to make up for the lack of timber the greens are very exacting and demand to be well read.

A packed gallery in front of the clubhouse watch the action at Inverness's 18th.

DID YOU KNOW?

At the British Open in 1920 the Inverness club set a precedent by opening its clubhouse doors to professional golfers, allowing them to use the locker room and other facilities. This was something the great Walter Hagen had been seeking for the professional for some years, and he showed his appreciation by making a collection among the professional golfers. They presented the club with a clock which was engraved:

God measures men by what they are
Not what in wealth they possess
The vibrant message chimes afar
The voice of Inverness

SCORECARD					
Hole	Yards	Par	Hole	Yards	Par
1	398	4	10	363	4
2	385	4	11	378	4
3	190	3	12	167	3
4	466	4	13	523	5
5	401	4	14	448	4
6	211	3	15	458	4
7	452	4	16	409	4
8	528	5	17	431	4
9	420	4	18	354	4
Out	3,451	35	In	3,531	36
TOTALS				6,982	71

MEDINAH

WHEN ASKED TO name the most difficult championship course in the United States, most leading professionals will say "Medinah." A look at the scores of the three Open champions at Medinah, 286, 287 and 280, will confirm that its 7,366-yard par-72 is far from easy. It is the longest course ever to be used for the US Open.

The championship course is the Old No. 3, and its tree-lined fairways and many doglegs add to its severity.

The hardest hole on the course is the 171-yard par-3 17th, which requires a drive over part of Lake Kadijah and also a bunker at the front of the green. It was at this hole that Sam Snead took three putts from the edge of the green during the 1949 US Open. He lost the title he never won by one stroke to Cary Middlecoff. Lou Graham won the 1975 Open at Medinah after a playoff with John Mahaffey in a tournament interrupted by a violent electrical storm. And in 1990 Hale Irwin

beat Mike Donald, also in a playoff. But what drama there was on the 72nd hole, when Irwin's 45-foot putt to force the playoff took seven seconds to make its journey from tee to hole.

The Medinah Club was founded in a Chicago suburb in the 1920s as a private club for the Shriners, or the Ancient Arabic Order of Nobles of the Mystic Shrine to give them their full title.

The Old No. 3 course was

SCORECARD					
Hole	Yards	Par	Hole	Yards	Par
1	388	4	10	582	5
2	184	3	11	407	4
3	415	4	12	471	4
4	447	4	13	219	3
5	530	5	14	583	5
6	449	4	15	389	4
7	589	5	16	452	4
8	206	3	17	171	3
9	439	4	18	445	4
Out	3,647	36	In	3,719	36
TOTALS				7,366	72

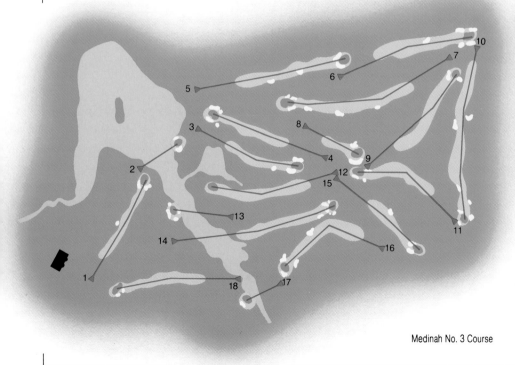

Medinah No. 3 Course

designed by Tom Bendelow, who intended laying the course out exclusively for women's use. However, at that time it was found to be too difficult for women's play, and it was taken over by the male members.

Bendelow's original design left

a lot to be desired, and many changes have been made over the years to bring this course up to championship standard. After Harry Cooper shot a 63 in winning the 1930 Medinah Open, and before Medinah staged its second US Open in 1975, George Fazio, who was beaten by Ben Hogan after a three-way playoff in the 50th Open at Merion in 1950, was called in to make further changes.

Hale Irwin teeing off while his partner Greg Norman waits at the 17th in the final round of the 1990 US Open at Medinah. Irwin beat Mike Donald in a playoff to capture the title.

MERION

THE MERION COURSE holds the distinction of staging more US Golf Association tournaments than any other course except for Augusta, which is the permanent home of the Masters.

Merion's long association with championship golf goes back to 1904, when it hosted the US Women's Amateur championship.

Situated at Ardmore, Pennsylvania, the club started life as the Merion Cricket Club in 1865. The first golf course was laid out on a leased piece of land at nearby Haverford in 1896. Originally a nine-hole course, it was expanded to 18 in 1900. Despite this, however, it was soon realized that it was too short and not demanding enough for championship golf. The club acquired a new piece of land at Ardmore, its present site, and in 1912 the new course was opened. This became known as the East Course. A second course was added in 1914.

The East Course, although less than 6,500 yards, is the one used for Championships. This must be a testament to its designer, Hugh Wilson, who created small, compact greens, well-guarded by bunkers. It was the first to be designed by Wilson, but he had spent many years studying championship courses and felt qualified to design his own. He was right.

There are only two par-fives at Merion, but coming in the first four holes, at the 2nd and 4th (600 yards), they offer a daunting

SCORECARD

Hole	Yards	Par	Hole	Yards	Par
1	362	4	10	310	4
2	536	5	11	369	4
3	181	3	12	371	4
4	600	5	13	127	3
5	418	4	14	408	4
6	420	4	15	366	4
7	350	4	16	428	4
8	360	4	17	220	3
9	179	3	18	463	4
Out	3,406	36	In	3,062	34
TOTALS				6,468	70

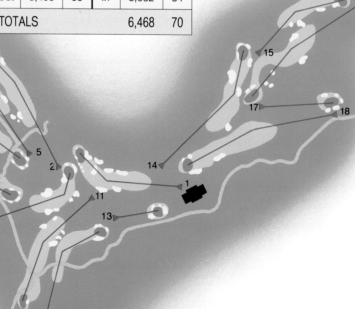

Merion East Course

It was Hogan's first Open since an horrific car accident in 1949 that nearly claimed his life. He was told by surgeons he would never walk again, let alone play golf. But, despite being in great discomfort, he achieved the impossible and captured the title.

Lee Trevino beat Jack Nicklaus in a playoff to win the 1971 Open at Merion, and ten years later Australia's David Graham became the first non-American winner since 1960.

Merion also witnessed one of golf's greatest occasions. It was here on September 27, 1930, that Bobby Jones completed his unique Grand Slam of the Open and Amateur titles of both Britain and the United States in one year. A plaque alongside the 11th hole commemorates his achievement.

Merion is notable in that the sticks do not have flags on them. Instead they have unique wicker baskets, which Hugh Wilson felt would make the course a bit harder, because players wouldn't be able to see which way the wind was blowing.

start to any round of golf. Wilson was a clever man, and the shortness of the course is more than compensated for by the strategically-placed bunkers and fast greens. The 8th is probably one of his finest holes. A bunker down the right awaits the short hitter, while the long hitter is faced with one to the left of the fairway.

Olin Dutra made up an eight-stroke deficit over the last two rounds to take the first Open at Merion in 1934. The club was honored with the 50th Open in 1950, and what an emotional championship it was, with Ben Hogan taking the title after a three-way playoff with George Fazio and Lloyd Mangrum.

Jerry Pate playing out of the monster bunker alongside Merion's 10th green.

One of Merion's beautiful greens.

MUIRFIELD VILLAGE

THE "COURSE THAT Jack Built," Muirfield Village was the brainchild of Jack Nicklaus and is named after the Scottish course where he won his first British Open in 1966. Jack has designed or helped in the design of many courses, but this is *his* course.

He first considered building his own course in 1966 and, naturally, wanted it to be in his home town of Columbus, Ohio, where Muirfield Village is situated. The idea came to him shortly after winning the Masters at Augusta, and he pictured it containing some of the beauty of the Augusta National. When he won the British Open three months later, the name for his course was chosen.

Despite attempts to talk him into taking his course to a more fashionable part of America, Nicklaus insisted on Columbus. After raising the necessary finance, he called in Peter Dye and Desmond Muirhead to advise with the design. Between them they came up with a course that is stiff enough to test the best of the world's professionals, but offers a fair chance to those people with double-figure handicaps.

They also gave consideration to the spectator in readiness for its use as a championship course, and many vantage points were created. Nicklaus, Dye, and Muirhead left nothing to chance. Yet, in search of perfection, the course has

SCORECARD					
Hole	Yards	Par	Hole	Yards	Par
1	446	4	10	441	4
2	452	4	11	538	5
3	392	4	12	156	3
4	204	3	13	442	4
5	531	5	14	363	4
6	430	4	15	490	5
7	549	5	16	204	3
8	189	3	17	430	4
9	410	4	18	437	4
Out	3,603	36	In	3,501	36
TOTALS				7,104	72

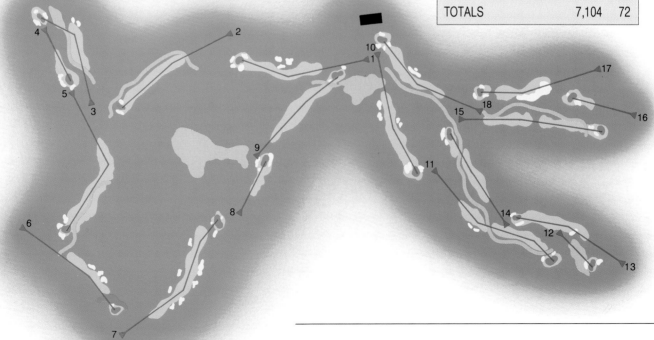

Above Muirfield Village has shades of Augusta about it. But that is hardly surprising in view of designer Jack Nicklaus's love of the Masters course.

undergone many changes over the years.

The Memorial Tournament is the one US Tour event played over Muirfield's 7,104-yard par-72 course. It first took place shortly after the course opened, in 1976, when Roger Maltbie beat Hale Irwin after a play-off. Nicklaus himself won the title in 1977, and again in 1984.

Jack's course hasn't been used for a Major, but in 1987 it was the venue for the Ryder Cup, and history was made there when the American team lost on home soil for the first time when Tony Jacklin's Europeans clinched a memorable 15-13 win.

Built into the course are many water hazards, which are an integral part of the modern golf course. The first five tees are all elevated, and most of the shots are downhillers. There are only two uphill shots on the whole course. The greens are superb, but one would expect that from a man like Nicklaus, who is an excellent putter. However, they are far from easy to play.

DID YOU KNOW?

The youngest player to score a hole-in-one was five-year-old Coby Orr at the Riverside Golf Course in San Antonio, Texas, in 1975. The youngest in Britain was six-year-old Mark Alexander of London, who aced the 109-yard 6th at Chessington, Surrey, in 1989.

139

OAK HILL

WHAT OAK HILL, in Rochester, New York, offers that many other championship courses do not is three closing holes that will reward the bold and brave, yet penalize those not so brave.

On this course, well-placed shots from the tee are essential, and these holes have ended many championship dreams in the past. The 16th is particularly evil. Trees line the right side of the fairway, while there is a slope to the left. Two bunkers guard the front of the 17th, and a fairway bunker catches many out at the 18th. But the approach to the green, which is set on a plateau, requires deadly accuracy, or the ball rolls away into a chasm below.

The large white bunkers were the idea of Robert Trent Jones, who re-designed a course originally laid out

by Donald Ross.

Oak Hill hosted its first US Open in 1956 when Cary Middlecoff took the title. Ben Hogan lost his chance to tie at the 17th when he attempted to clear those two greenside bunkers, which he did, only to see his ball roll off the green.

Lee Trevino equaled the Open record with a 275 when he won Oak Hill's second Open in 1968. And in 1989 Curtis Strange became the first man for 38 years to win back-to-back Opens. Jack Nicklaus, in 1980, won the only US PGA Championship to be played at Oak Hill.

The 18th at Oak Hill with its very difficult approach.

Hole	Yards	Par	Hole	Yards	Par
1	377	4	10	408	4
2	436	4	11	479	5
3	420	4	12	303	4
4	145	3	13	448	4
5	381	4	14	210	3
6	543	5	15	413	4
7	442	4	16	474	5
8	156	3	17	208	3
9	365	4	18	441	4
Out	3,265	35	In	3,384	36
TOTALS				6,649	71

SCORECARD

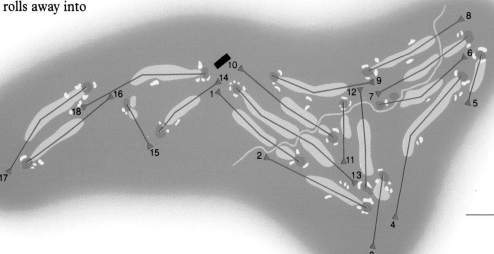

OAKLAND HILLS

OAKLAND HILLS, SITUATED in Birmingham, near Detroit, Michigan, is not one of America's most attractive courses, but it offers a varied and stiff test to the golfer.

Shortly before the 1951 US Open at Oakland Hills, the US Golf Association called for the club to make the course a sterner test of the professionals' ability.

Robert Trent Jones was called in, and the course was revamped and modernized. Jones made the fairways narrower, made the rough more severe, and increased the number of bunkers to more than 100. The best golf was needed to get anything like par.

Donald Ross designed the original course which was opened in 1918, and the club's first professional, albeit for 12 months, was none other than Walter Hagen. The natural surroundings were ideal for a golf course.

The US Open first came to Oakland Hills in 1924 when English-born Cyril Walker carried off the title. Ralph Guldahl won in 1937 with a record score of 281. Hogan was the champion at

One of Oakland Hills' large greens, well protected by bunkers.

Oakland Hills in 1951, and Gene Littler in 1961. Andy North was champion when the Open was last played there in 1985.

The course has become slightly easier, but it still remains a tough test. The last five holes are the climax and can catch out the unsuspecting golfer at a time when his concentration may just be slipping.

In addition to staging five US Opens, it has twice staged the US Seniors Championship and in 1972 and 1979 hosted the PGA Championship which, coincidentally, were won by two

non-Americans, Gary Player of South Africa and Australia's David Graham.

It was Player who played one of Oakland Hills' most memorable shots on his way to winning the title in 1972. Having sliced his tee shot at the 16th at a time when any one of six men could have taken the title, he took a nine-iron from the rough and sent the ball 150 yards over the lake and to within three feet of the pin. He made a birdie, and the title was his for the taking.

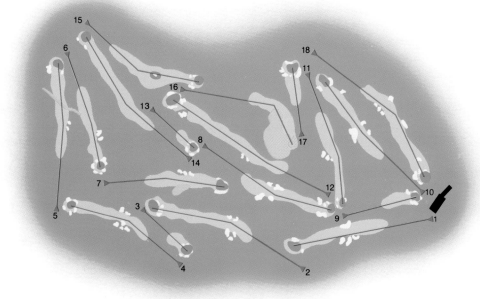

SCORECARD					
Hole	Yards	Par	Hole	Yards	Par
1	436	4	10	454	4
2	527	5	11	411	4
3	199	3	12	560	5
4	433	4	13	172	3
5	457	4	14	465	4
6	359	4	15	399	4
7	405	4	16	409	4
8	439	4	17	201	3
9	217	3	18	453	4
Out	3,472	35	In	3,524	35
TOTALS				6,996	70

OAKMONT

THE OAKMONT COUNTRY Club near Pittsburgh, Pennsylvania, has hosted the US Open on six occasions. Only Baltusrol has staged it as many times.

Tommy Armour won Oakmont's first Open in 1927, and the last winner was Larry Nelson in 1983. On the third day that year, a record crowd for one day at the Open, 38,046, paid to watch the battle between the eventual runner-up Tom Watson and Spain's Severiano Ballesteros.

Oakmont is a test of nerve as well as skill. Players have Henry C. Fownes, a local industrialist who devised and laid out the original course in 1903, to thank for that. Nearly 200 bunkers add to its severity (there were about 220 on the original course), and the greens are regarded as the fastest in the U.S. One of the many bunkers is the infamous Church Pews bunker which measures 40 yards by 60 yards and has nine smaller bunkers within the main one!

Oakmont is regarded as the most difficult 18 holes of golf in the United States. But in winning the 1973 US Open, Johnny Miller humiliated the course with a record 63 in the final round which,

in rain-soaked conditions, was a magnificent achievement. It is widely held to be one of the finest rounds ever witnessed in America.

Oakmont's first major championship was the 1919 US Amateur Championship. The beaten finalist that day was Bobby Jones. When it was next held there, Jones became champion.

Work on Oakmont started in the fall of 1903, and within six weeks the first 12 holes were

The beautiful, if not demanding, 5th at Oakmont.

completed. Fownes' dream of creating "the hardest golf course it was possible to design" was well underway. The following fall, all 18 holes were ready for play.

In 1987 Oakmont became a National Historic Landmark, the only golf course in the United States to be so designated.

SCORECARD					
Hole	Yards	Par	Hole	Yards	Par
1	469	4	10	462	4
2	343	4	11	371	4
3	425	4	12	603	5
4	561	5	13	185	3
5	379	4	14	360	4
6	201	3	15	453	4
7	434	4	16	228	3
8	240	3	17	322	4
9	480	5	18	456	4
Out	3,532	36	In	3,440	35
TOTALS				6,972	71

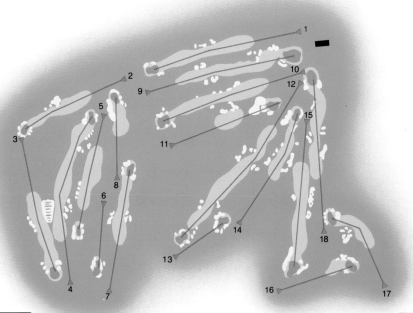

OLYMPIC CLUB

WHEREFORE YOU LOOK at the Olympic Club on the western edge of San Francisco, you can see nothing but trees. In fact the course is adorned with approximately 30,000 of them.

At the turn of the century, the site was mostly sand dunes and had virtually no trees. Now, some of them are over 100 feet tall. The site is between Lake Merced and the Pacific Ocean. However, despite its proximity, the ocean cannot be seen from the Lakeside Course - hardly surprising, with all those trees!

However, the other course, the Ocean Course, commands some breathtaking views across the ocean. But it is not suitable for championship golf.

A shortage of bunkers, fairway, and greenside, gives the impression the course is easy. It is not. The par-4s offer a great deal of variety and reaching them in regulation two offers the toughest of tests even for the professionals. In the 3rd hole, the Lakeside Course has one of the great golf holes. It is not hard - it is a 223-yard downhill par-3. But standing on the elevated tee, you have breathtaking views of San Francisco and the Golden Gate Bridge.

The moist San Francisco atmosphere reduces carry and roll which is something many new-comers overlook.

It was at the Olympic in 1966 that Arnold Palmer threw away a seemingly invincible lead of seven shots in the Open, before making a remarkable comeback at the 18th from deep rough to force a play-off with Billy Casper - only to lose by four shots the next day!

What a magnificent sight! A packed crowd around the 8th watching Bernhard Langer in action during the 1987 US Open at the Olympic Club. Scott Simpson was the surprise winner.

The 18th at Olympic is one of golf's great spectator holes. The small green sits in the corner of a horseshoe-shaped fairway set in a dip, giving wonderful banked vantage points.

SCORECARD					
Hole	Yards	Par	Hole	Yards	Par
1	533	5	10	422	4
2	394	4	11	430	4
3	223	3	12	390	4
4	438	4	13	186	3
5	457	4	14	417	4
6	437	4	15	149	3
7	288	4	16	609	5
8	137	3	17	522	5
9	433	4	18	343	4
Out	3,340	35	In	3,468	36
TOTALS				6,808	71

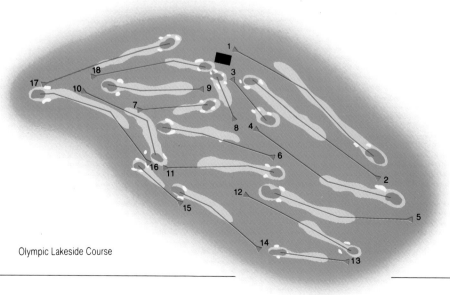

Olympic Lakeside Course

PEBBLE BEACH

FOR A COMBINATION of beauty, the spectacular, and an exciting golf course, Pebble Beach stands head and shoulders above the rest.

Situated on the Monterey peninsula approximately 120 miles south of San Francisco, it was the first of many superb golf courses to be built in the area. The others, Cypress Point, Monterey and Spyglass Hill, all followed later.

Pebble Beach was opened in 1919 and was the idea of Samuel Morse, the nephew of the man who invented Morse code. Morse bought the land from the Southern Pacific Railroad Company, and to help him develop the course he obtained the services of Jack Neville who, surprisingly, was *not* a golf course designer, but a real estate salesman. Nevertheless, they produced an excellent golf course spreading from the cliffs along the coastline inland to the edge of the Del Monte Forest.

The 7th hole ranks as one of the most beautiful, and certainly most photographed, holes in the world.

It is a par-3 measuring little over 100 yards. But what a setting! The green is set on its own, jutting out into the Pacific Ocean. But there are other great holes at Pebble Beach. The second shot to the 8th requires a carry over a 100-foot drop into the Ocean

Above Pebble Beach's 18th hole is probably one of the toughest closing holes in Championship golf.

Left One of golf's most photographed holes, the 7th at Pebble Beach.

below. And the 18th along the rocky coastline is probably one of the best finishing holes in golf. To any championship-winning aspirant, the task of making par at each of the last two holes is one of the most daunting prospects in the game.

Tom Watson tore those last two holes apart when winning his first US Open in 1982. He required two pars to force a play-off with Jack Nicklaus, but birdies gave him the title by two strokes.

That was only the second time Pebble Beach had played host to the US Open; its location, 120 miles from the nearest big city, has limited its use as a Major venue.

It first hosted the Open in 1972 when Jack Nicklaus won his third title, and it played host for a third time in 1992. Lanny Wadkins captured his first Major, the PGA Championship, at Pebble Beach in 1977.

Despite only holding four Majors, the Californian course is one of the three used for the AT&T National Pro-Am, which is one of the US Tour events each year. It was previously known as the Bing Crosby Pro-Am.

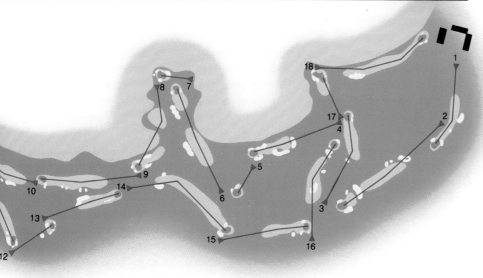

SCORECARD

Hole	Yards	Par	Hole	Yards	Par
1	373	4	10	426	4
2	502	5	11	384	4
3	388	4	12	202	3
4	327	4	13	392	4
5	166	3	14	565	5
6	516	5	15	397	4
7	107	3	16	402	4
8	431	4	17	209	3
9	464	4	18	548	5
Out	3,274	36	In	3,525	36
TOTALS				6,799	72

PINEHURST

THERE ARE SEVEN courses at Pinehurst in North Carolina, but by far the best is the No. 2 course.

The inaugural nine-hole course was laid out in 1898 by James Tufts, a Boston pharmacist. He had previously acquired a 5,000 acre site, so land was no problem. A year later, the course was extended to 18 holes, and after Harry Vardon played the course during his visit to the U.S. in 1900, golf took off in the area. It was then that Tufts called for the services of Scotsman Donald Ross.

Ross arrived to take up duties as golfing coach in 1900, but most of his time was spent designing four more courses for the area.

The No. 2 was completed in 1907 and in 1910 the No. 3 course arrived on the scene. When No. 4 was opened in 1919, Pinehurst became the first American club to have four courses. But it went one better in 1950 when the fifth course was opened shortly after Ross's death. Since then, two more courses have been added, and Pinehurst can rightly claim to be the biggest golfing center in the U.S.

Pinehurst staged the PGA Championship in 1936, its only Major, when Denny Shute beat Jimmy Thomson in the final. Since then, the biggest event to be played over the North Carolina course was the 1951 Ryder Cup.

The World Golf Hall of Fame is situated at Pinehurst and was inaugurated in 1974 by President Gerald Ford, himself a keen golfer. Between 1903 and 1950, Pinehurst hosted the North and South Open, and it was here in 1940 that Ben Hogan won his first ever US Tour event.

SCORECARD

Hole	Yards	Par	Hole	Yards	Par
1	373	4	10	454	5
2	167	3	11	335	4
3	340	4	12	137	3
4	526	5	13	360	4
5	372	4	14	372	4
6	361	4	15	478	5
7	353	4	16	314	4
8	486	5	17	178	3
9	120	3	18	402	4
Out	3,098	36	In	3,030	36
TOTALS				6,128	72

Pinehurst No. 2 Course

Although Pinehurst is a challenging course, it is not used as a Championship course because of its rural location.

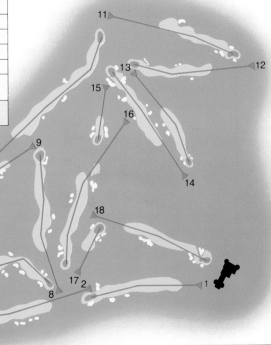

146

PINE VALLEY

PINE VALLEY IS one of the truly spectacular golf courses, with its 2nd hole being one of the game's great holes.

It is only a 367-yard par-4, but as you stand on the tee looking at the green, the fairway is littered with bunkers. The view is spectacular and the temptation is to photograph the fairway rather than attempt to play it.

But the 2nd is just one of 18 holes at Pine Valley with its own individual characteristics adding to the overall beauty of the course.

Located in Clementon, New Jersey, the course was originally developed by George Crump, owner of the Colonnades Hotel in Philadelphia, who wanted to fulfill a dream of building the best and toughest golf course in the world. He was assisted in the design by British architect H. S. Colt, and they developed the course around a previously untouched 184 acres of forest area in southern New Jersey. The sandy soil made design a lot easier.

Crump is said to have spotted the land while making a train journey from Philadelphia to Atlantic City and immediately decided it was the location for his "dream." The land was once the home of an encampment occupied by the Delaware Indians.

In 1912 Crump persuaded 18 friends to invest $1,000 each, and they purchased the land.

The course opened in 1916 as a 14-hole course and was immediately hailed as one of the most demanding in the U.S., if not the world. That is a belief many golfers still hold today, as accuracy to avoid the bunkers and trees is crucial at every hole. It became a full 18-hole course in 1919, but Crump never lived to see the completion of his dream. He had died the previous year.

What makes Pine Valley tougher than most courses is the lack of fairways. Each tee shot has to land on a predetermined area which, in most cases, is large enough to hit. But poor shots are heavily penalized because of the severe rough.

Fear hits you the first time you play Pine Valley. Just looking around at the trees and bunkers is enough to make you want to put your clubs away and spend the day playing the 19th hole 18 times instead!

Club members are willing to take bets that nobody, amateur or professional, will break 80 the first time they play Pine Valley.

Despite its beautiful setting, Pine Valley is still waiting to host its first Major.

SCORECARD					
Hole	Yards	Par	Hole	Yards	Par
1	427	4	10	146	3
2	367	4	11	392	4
3	181	3	12	344	4
4	444	4	13	448	4
5	232	3	14	184	3
6	388	4	15	591	5
7	567	5	16	433	4
8	319	4	17	338	4
9	427	4	18	428	4
Out	3,352	35	In	3,304	35
TOTALS				6,656	70

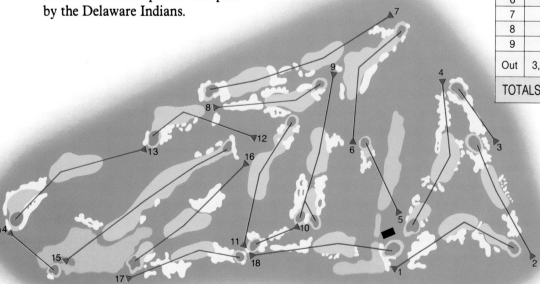

147

SHINNECOCK HILLS

FORMED IN 1891, Shinnecock Hills has been in existence ever since and, consequently, is one of the longest-surviving clubs in the United States.

Scotsman Willie Dunn laid out the original course, and on its completion he became the club's first professional. Dunn's original course was styled on Scottish design, and his ancestry is very evident.

Situated at Southampton, Long Island, Shinnecock Hills can boast the oldest clubhouse in the United States, dating back to 1892. It was also the first 18-hole course in the U.S. The course is named after the Shinnecock tribe of Indians who once lived in the area.

It hosted the second US Open in 1896, but it had to wait ninety years to stage its next championship. On that occasion Raymond Floyd became the oldest

Above A view of the 9th and 18th greens at Shinnecock Hills, the first 18-hole golf course in the United States.

Right A superb view across the Shinnecock Hills links with the 18th, the "Home" hole in the foreground.

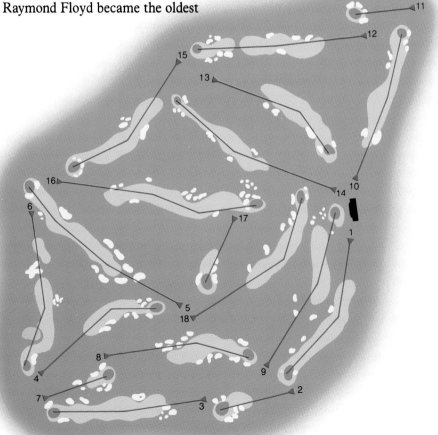

SCORECARD					
Hole	Yards	Par	Hole	Yards	Par
1	391	4	10	412	4
2	221	3	11	158	3
3	456	4	12	469	4
4	382	4	13	366	4
5	512	5	14	447	4
6	456	4	15	400	4
7	184	3	16	519	5
8	361	4	17	169	3
9	411	4	18	426	4
Out	3,374	35	In	3,366	35
TOTALS				6,740	70

champion ever, at 43 years and 284 days.

The idea of a golf course in New York came when William Vanderbilt saw Dunn play an exhibition match in Biarritz. Upon his return to New York, the millionaire discussed his plans with friends, and when they decided to go ahead, he contacted Dunn, who made the trip across the Atlantic.

Dunn set about looking for a suitable site, which he found set among sandhills close to the sea. It was reminiscent of the east coast of Scotland where he had lived.

The course was ready for use in the summer of 1891, and when Stanford White was called in to design a luxurious clubhouse, Shinnecock Hills rightly claimed

to be the best golf club in the United States.

As the game gained in popularity, so did the exclusivity of the Shinnecock Hills Club, and members had to wear red coats when playing - a rule that had existed in Britain in the early days of golf.

While some of the present-day course bears some of Dunn's traits, a lot of it now dates to the early 1930s, when Dick Wilson made many changes because its length of only 5,000 yards was far too short for the game in the 1930s, and it certainly would not gain championship status again unless changes were made. The final hole, perhaps the toughest on the course, certainly bears a

resemblance to Dunn's early design; it is very British with an undulating fairway, severe rough on both sides, and with a strong wind often blowing across it.

SHINNECOCK HILLS' 18 HOLES	
1 Westward Ho!	10 Eastward Ho!
2 Plateau	11 Hill Head
3 Peconic	12 Tuckahoe
4 Pump House	13 Road Side
5 Montauk	14 Thom's Elbow
6 The Pond	15 Sebonac
7 Redan	16 Shinnecock
8 Lowlands	17 Eden
9 Ben Nevis	18 Home

WINGED FOOT

WINGED FOOT IS one of the best-known courses in the United States. Situated in Mamaroneck, north of New York, it was founded in the 1920s by members of the New York Athletic Club, and it was from their emblem that the club's name was taken.

The club boasts two 18-hole courses, East and West, and while it is the longer West Course which is used for championship golf, many members prefer the East Course. Architect A.W. Tillinghast had the responsibility of designing the course, and in doing so he game the New York Athletic Club members something to think about, because the West Course was one of the toughest in the United States. Both opened in 1923.

What makes Winged Foot particularly difficult is the length of the par-4s. Seven of them are over 440 yards, and even the best players sometimes have difficulty in reaching the greens in the regulation number of strokes.

The US Open was first played at Winged Foot in 1929, when Bobby Jones captured his third title. His score of 14 *over* par certainly highlights how severe the West Course was. When Billy Casper became the second Open champion at Winged Foot, 30 years later, he needed to single putt no fewer than 31 greens in order to keep his score *down* to 282. It was during Casper's triumph that violent thunderstorms caused the match to be delayed for a day for the first time in Open history.

Hale Irwin beat a very difficult course to win after a playoff in 1974, and in 1984 another playoff was required as Fuzzy Zoeller beat Greg Norman.

For many years, Jack Nicklaus maintained that Winged Foot's 17th was the greatest match of a golfer's skill against that of the designer. It requires a long accurate drive amid trees, followed by a long second shot to a green well-protected by bunkers.

Right Fuzzy Zoeller, Greg Norman, and a very large crowd around the 13th green during the 1984 US Open at Winged Foot. Zoeller beat Norman by eight strokes in a playoff to take his first title.

Below right Zoeller playing out of a bunker on his way to winning his title in 1984.

SCORECARD					
Hole	Yards	Par	Hole	Yards	Par
1	446	4	10	190	3
2	411	4	11	386	4
3	216	3	12	535	5
4	453	4	13	212	3
5	515	5	14	418	4
6	324	4	15	417	4
7	166	3	16	457	4
8	442	4	17	449	4
9	471	4	18	448	4
Out	3,444	35	In	3,512	35
TOTALS				6,956	70

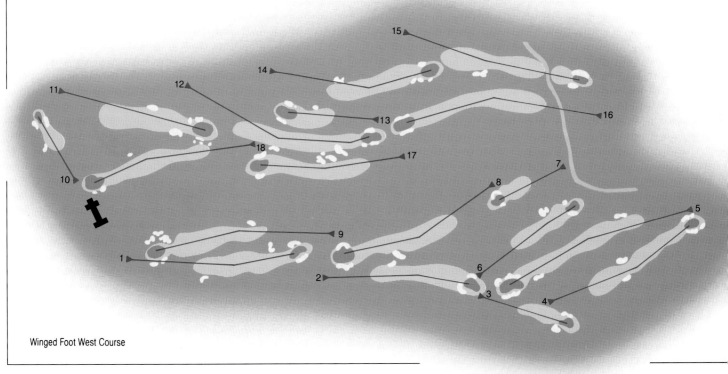

Winged Foot West Course

GOLFING TERMINOLOGY

IT IS IMPORTANT with golf that you familiarize yourself with the rules of the game and, just as important, the rules of etiquette. You always stand a chance of getting onto a golf course anywhere in the world, no matter how high your handicap. But if you do not adhere to the rules of general etiquette you will not be made welcome.

The rules of golf are lengthy and very complicated. To condense them would not do them justice, and so the best advice is to get hold of a copy of these rules from any good bookshop. You could write direct to the United States Golf Association, Far Hills, New Jersey, or the Royal and Ancient, St. Andrews, Scotland.

It is also important that you familiarize yourself with some golfing terminology that will crop up regularly. Birdies, pars, eagles, and albatrosses are terms that are often used, and there are many others which will be described here in detail.

ACE See *Hole-in-One.*

ADDRESS Once a player has taken up his *stance* and *grounded* the clubhead behind the ball, he or she is said to have addressed the ball. Note that the clubhead must *not* be grounded in a *bunker.*

AIR SHOT A shot played at the ball, that misses. It counts as one *stroke.* Also known as the *air stroke.*

ALBATROSS A score of three strokes *under par* for a *hole.* An albatross is very rare, even among the leading professionals. Also known as a *Double Eagle.*

APPROACH A shot made from the *fairway* onto, or toward, the *green.*

APRON The area surrounding the

green that is cut shorter than the *fairway,* but not quite as short as the *putting surface.* Also known as the *fringe.*

BACK NINE The last nine holes of an 18-hole round. Also known as the *Inward Half.*

BACKSWING A very important part of the golf swing. It is when the clubhead is taken away from its *address* position to the top of the arc, before the *downswing* and eventual contact with the ball. If the backswing is wrong, then there is little chance of getting the rest of the *swing* right.

BEST BALL A form of competition when one player competes against two or three others and the score of the individual player is matched against the best score of the other players. It can be adapted to both *match* and *medal play* golf.

BETTER BALL A match involving four players, two on each side, and the better ball of each pair counts at each hole. Again it can be used in *match* or *medal play* conditions.

BIRDIE A score of one stroke *under par* for a *hole.*

BOGEY (a) One stroke *over par* for a *hole.* A double bogey is two over par and triple bogey three over par. (b) The number of strokes a good player is expected to need to complete one hole, or the complete round.

BUNKER A mound or sand-filled hollow strategically placed on the course - normally where you want to hit your ball! Also known as a *trap.* The rules state that you must not *ground* your clubhead during *address* when in a bunker and, as a matter of courtesy to other golfers, all marks made by the golfer in a bunker must be raked over on leaving it.

CARRY The distance covered by the golf ball from the point where it was hit to the point where it first lands.

CASUAL WATER A temporary accumulation of water on the golf course. A player may move his ball from casual water without penalty.

CHIP A low trajectory/lofted shot normally over some form of obstacle - bunker, tree, water, etc. - and usually made onto or toward the *green.*

CLOSED STANCE A position in which a right-handed player's left

---

DID YOU KNOW?

It is believed that the birdie *was so named when Abe Smith, playing in Atlantic City at the turn of the 20th century, played his second shot to a par-4 within inches of the hole. He then turned to his playing partners and said: "That was one bird of a shot."*

The term "eagle" *was also first used in the United States, but not until the 1920s; and, because the eagle is a splendid bird, it was appropriately used to describe a hole played in one stroke better than a plain birdie. For the same reason, albatross was probably chosen to describe a hole played in one stroke better than an eagle.*

foot is slightly in front of the right one at *address*.

CUT A type of spin imparted on the ball which causes it to travel to the right. It is often the cause of the slice. Also the term used when the field in a tournament is reduced from its original number. In most professional tournaments, the field is cut after 54 and 72 holes.

DIVOT A piece of turf cut out of the ground while playing a shot. Divots are usually cut with lofted clubs like 9-irons and wedges when trying to impart backspin on the ball. Divots must be replaced, and if you are walking the course and find an unplaced divot, don't walk past it - replace it. If every player did that once on every round, golf courses would be in much better condition.

DOGLEG A *fairway* that has a change of direction between *tee* and *green* is described as a dogleg.

DORMIE In *match play* golf, a player or team is said to be dormie when they cannot lose. If, for example, they are leading by two holes and there are two holes to play then they are said to be "dormie two."

DOUBLE EAGLE See *Albatross*.

DOWNSWING Following the *takeaway* of the club from the *address* position to the top of the *backswing*, the next action is the downswing which, like all other aspects of the *swing*, is very important.

DRAW A controlled shot that makes the ball travel initially to the right of the target, but then deliberately turn left toward it.

DRIVE A shot made from the *tee*, usually with a driver or other wood, although many of today's professionals tend to drive with long irons.

DROPPING THE BALL During a round, a player may have to relocate his ball, either because it is unplayable, or it has landed on ground under repair and must be moved so as not to cause damage. The rules governing the dropping of a ball are very strict. At one time the drop was made from over the player's shoulder; now it is made with an outstretched arm in front of the player.

EAGLE Two shots *under par* for a *hole*.

FADE A controlled shot like the *draw*, but with the ball initially veering left of its target before turning right toward it.

FAIRWAY The area between *tee* and *green*. Both sides of the fairway are often bound by natural hazards such as trees, bushes, or long grass known as the *rough*. The fairway is the mown area between the tee and the green, but it is not cut as short as the green.

FLIGHT OF THE BALL As its name implies, the path taken by the ball while in flight. There are many different flight paths the ball can take. There is *straight flight*, *slice* and *hook*, *push* and *pull*, and *draw* and *fade*.

FOLLOW-THROUGH The action of allowing the clubhead to continue its *swing* after making contact with the ball.

FORE! A warning shout made by golfers to fellow golfers on the course that a ball may be heading toward them.

FOUR BALL A match involving four players, usually playing in pairs. The better ball of each pair

can decide each *hole,* or the aggregate scores can decide the winners.

FOURSOMES A match involving four players divided into two teams who use one ball each and take turns to play shots at their respective ball.

FRINGE See *apron*.

FRONT NINE The first nine holes of an 18-hole round. Also known as the *Outward Half.*

GIMMIE A term used when a player allows his opponent a *putt* without playing the ball himself. It is a sporting gesture and usually made when there is little danger of the putt being missed.

GREEN The finely manicured *putting surface* which one aims to reach in the least number of strokes from the *teeing* area. Greens are well cared for and must be treated with respect. Don't take *pull carts* onto the green, replace all *pitch* marks made by balls landing on the green, and, like *divots,* if you see an unrepaired pitch mark, don't leave it, repair it.

GRIP The part of the club shaft that is held by the golfer. The hold you take on the club is also referred to as "the grip."

GROSS SCORE The score achieved by a player in a *strokeplay* or *medalplay* round before his *handicap* is deducted.

GROUNDING THE CLUB Once the clubhead has been placed on the ground behind the ball at *address* it is said to be grounded.

GROUND UNDER REPAIR Golf courses are continuously undergoing repair to make them better places to play on. GUR areas are appropriately marked, and balls landing therein must be removed, but without penalty.

HALVE, TO In *match play* to play a *hole* in the same number of strokes as the opposing player or team results in the hole being "halved."

HANDICAPPING Handicap systems vary so much from club-to-club and country-to-country that it

would be impossible to analyze them in such a short space. However, if you take up the sport seriously, you should ask at your local club about obtaining an official handicap. Without one you will not be able to compete in many competitions and tournaments.

HAZARDS The rules of golf describe a hazard as a *bunker* or water hazard only. But other things like roads, walls, trees, bushes, etc. are certainly hazardous if you come across them during a round of golf.

HOLE That 4¼in. (12cm) diameter target that is cut into the *green*, which all golfers are striving to reach in the least number of shots. As the hole's position on the green is changed frequently, its position is shown by a flag on a pole, so players can see where to play their *approach* shots.

HOLE-IN-ONE Playing a shot from the *tee* that goes directly into the hole. Normally done only at *par*-3 *holes*, but a hole-in-one has been recorded at a 447-yard par-4 hole. Also known as an *Ace*.

HOLING OUT The final act of putting the ball into the *hole*.

HONOR The rules dictate that the person or team winning the previous *hole* has the "honor" of going first at the next hole. If the hole is halved, then the person having the honor at the previous hole retains it.

HOOK A hooked shot is generally caused as a result of an error. The ball heads toward the target before changing direction and heading well left of the intended target.

IN PLAY A ball is in play from the moment it is struck from the *teeing* area.

INWARD HALF The last nine holes of an 18-hole round of golf. Also known as the *Back Nine*.

LATERAL WATER HAZARD Lateral water hazards are marked with red marker posts and are water hazards that run parallel to the fairway, thus making it impossible to drop the ball behind the hazard under normal rules. In the case of lateral water hazards, the ball must be dropped within two club lengths of where it entered the hazard, but not nearer to the *hole*.

LIE The position where the ball comes to rest.

LINKS Strictly speaking, any area where golf is played can be termed the "links." But it is generally a term used to define only a golf course adjacent to the coast.

LOCAL RULES All golf clubs, in addition to the recognized Rules of Golf, have Local Rules which must be obeyed. Local Rules are printed on scorecards and must be read before a round.

LOST BALL A ball is deemed to be lost if not found within five minutes of starting to look for it.

MATCH PLAY A form of competition whereby one team or individual attempts to win more *holes* than the other. The person or team winning a hole goes one up, two up, and so on until there are not enough holes left for the opponent to be able to win. Halved holes do not affect the score.

MEDAL PLAY The simplest form of competition whereby each player's, or team's, aggregate strokes for the round are calculated, and the appropriate deductions are then made for *handicap(s)*.

DID YOU KNOW?

The longest recorded hole-in-one was achieved by Robert Mitera at the appropriately named Miracle Hill golf course at Omaha, Nebraska in 1965. A two-handicap player, Mitera's drive at the 409m (447yd) downhill 10th hole landed in the hole. He was aided by a tailwind!

NET SCORE A player's score after the deduction of his *handicap* from his gross score.

OFF SCRATCH A player is said to be "off scratch" when he or she plays to a handicap of zero.

OPEN STANCE An open stance is when a right-handed player's left foot is drawn back slightly from the line of flight.

OUT OF BOUNDS Certain areas of a golf course are designated as Out of Bounds and are indicated by white marker posts. Any ball that goes out of bounds must be replayed at the position from which it was originally played, with the addition of a one-stroke penalty.

OUTWARD HALF The first nine holes of an 18-hole round of golf. Also known as the *Front Nine*.

OVER PAR A score of more than the *par* figure for a *hole* or round.

PAR The par figure for each hole. It is the score with which an expert golfer would be expected to complete it. Length decides *par* figures and assumes that top players would two *putt* on each green so, for example, it would be assumed a leading professional would reach a 197-yard green in one shot and then two putt. It would therefore be designated a par-3.

PIN HIGH A ball is pin high when it is level with the flag, but either to the right or left of it.

PITCH A shot played with a lofted club high into the air so that the ball lands on the *green*. Depending on conditions, the ball will either stop dead on hitting the *putting surface*, or will land and then run on after pitching. The softer the putting surface, the more chance

there is of the ball stopping dead.

PITCH MARK When a ball is hit with a lofted club toward the *green*, it will leave a pitch mark in the green upon landing. Always repair any pitch marks your ball makes.

PLUGGED BALL A ball that remains in its own *pitch mark* is said to be plugged. This happens most often in *bunkers*, but can also happen on *fairways* if they are very soft after rain.

PREFERRED LIES During the winter months, but occasionally at other times, the local rules will state that preferred lies are allowed on the *fairways*. This rule is to protect the fairway from undue wear in bad weather; your ball can be moved to a good piece of ground, normally within one club-length of its original landing place, but not nearer to the *hole*.

PULL A shot that flies to the left but, unlike the *hook*, does not start by going to the right first.

PULL CART An aid for carrying the golf bag around the course. Many clubs offer cart rental, and many clubs have electric carts to rent as well.

PUSH A shot that goes to the right but, unlike the *slice*, does not start by going to the left first.

PUTT The action of attempting to get the ball into the hole from on the *putting surface* by using the putter.

PUTTING GREEN (PUTTING SURFACE) The correct name for the *green*.

RECEIVE A BYE To be exempt from an early round of a competition, thus going straight into a later round.

ROUGH The uncut area adjacent to the *fairway*. The first bit of rough is usually the "light rough" or "semi-rough," while the remainder is the "deep rough."

SHAFT The part of the golf club between the handle and the clubhead.

SLICE A sliced shot is usually the result of an error. The ball heads toward the target before changing direction and heading well to the right of its intended target.

STABLEFORD A form of competition based on a points system which allows one point for a *hole* played in one *stroke* over *par*, two points if played in par, three points for a *birdie*, four for an *eagle*, and five for an *albatross*.

STANCE The position a player adopts when addressing the ball. It is very important to make sure the correct stance is adopted.

STROKE A stroke is when the club is moved forward with the intention of hitting the ball. If it does not hit it (see *Air Shot*), it still counts as one stroke.

STRAIGHT FLIGHT When the ball travels in a straight line while in flight.

STROKE INDEX Each *hole* is graded according to its stroke index and is clearly indicated on the scorecard. The most difficult hole on the course is stroke 1 while the easiest is stroke 18.

STROKE PLAY Another name for *medal play.*

SWING The swing is the most important part of the game of golf. A bad swing will almost certainly result in bad golf. The swing is the action of taking the club away from the *address* position, up through the *backswing*, into the *downswing*, and then into contact with the ball.

TAKEAWAY The first movement of

the clubhead when it is taken away from the ball at the *address* position.

TEE The small plastic or wooden peg on which the ball is placed when playing from *the tee.*

TENDING THE FLAG When putting on the putting surface, the flag must be taken *out* of the hole before the ball enters it. However, if the ball is a fair distance from the hole, the flag may be left in and tended by another player who must make sure it is removed before the ball enters the hole.

THE TEE Normally raised, it is a clearly marked area. Each *hole* begins from the tee. Ladies have tees in front of the men's, and there is normally a third tee behind each hole set aside for competitions. Two markers clearly indicate the place from which tee shots must be played; they must be from between and behind the markers. Pull carts and golf bags should not be taken onto the tee.

THREESOME A match when one player plays against two others who take shots in turn at the same ball.

TOPPED BALL A ball is "topped" when the top half, instead of the bottom half, is struck with the club. The most common cause for topping a ball is a player moving his or her head during the *swing.*

TOUR A series of tournaments, usually spread over a full season, for professional golfers. There are Tours in many different parts of the world, but the US PGA Tour and the PGA European Tour are the two biggest.

TRAP See *bunker.*

UNDER PAR A score of fewer strokes than the *par* figure for a *hole* or round.

WATER HAZARDS The Rules of Golf define a water hazard as any "sea, lake, pond, river, ditch, surface drainage ditch, or other open water course, whether it contains water or not, and anything of a similar nature." Water hazards are marked by yellow posts or lines. (See also *Lateral Water Hazard.*)

WINTER GREEN To protect the greens in the winter months, temporary greens are often cut out of the *fairway.* They are not manicured as well as the normal greens, but without them many courses would be forced to close during the winter.

DID YOU KNOW?

The special prize for a hole-in-one at the 8th hole during the 1985 New South Wales Open was either £5,000 in cash, or a pre-paid funeral with a monument. The prize was offered by local PGA director, and funeral parlour owner, Paul Smith . . . it is not known whether the event went to a sudden death play-off!

CONVERSION TABLE

Both imperial and metric measurements have been used throughout the book as these vary from one golf club to another. To help you convert measurements please see the table below.

Meters	Yards
100	110
150	164
200	219
250	273
300	328
350	383
400	437
450	492
500	547
550	601
600	656
650	711
700	766
750	820
800	875
850	930
900	984
950	1039
1000	1094
2000	2187
3000	3281
4000	4374
5000	5468

INDEX

ACKNOWLEDGMENTS

Quarto would like to thank the following for providing photographs, and for permission to reproduce copyright material. While every effort has been made to trace and acknowledge all copyright holders, we would like to apologize should there have been any omissions.

Key: (t) = top; (b) = below; (l) = left; (r) = right; (m) = middle; (both) = both photographs on the page.

Baltusrol Golf Club, page: 129 (both).

Peter Dazeley Golf Photography, pages: 33, 37, 43, 44(l), 45(t), 48(t), 49(tr), 50(both), 51(both), 53(r), 54(l), 55(b), 57(both), 58, 60(tr & b both), 61(r), 63(t), 65(b), 67, 70(t), 70(bl), 74, 77, 78(br), 79(l), 81(b), 90, 92(b), 96(both), 97, 98, 99, 100, 101(t), 112, 114, 116(t), 117, 119(t), 121(r), 126(b), 130, 131, 144, 145.

Mansell Collection, pages: 8(t), 9, 10.

Mark Newcombe/ Visions in Golf, pages: 7, 8(both), 11, 12, 14(l), 15(t), 15(m & b), 16, 28, 34, 35, 41, 44(r), 45(b), 46(b), 47(l), 48(br), 49(b), 52(b), 54(both), 16, 58-9, 60(tl), 61(t & bl), 62, 63(b), 64, 68(t), 69(both), 72(t), 73, 82(r), 75(all three), 76, 79(r), 92, 93, 94, 95(all three), 101(b), 102, 103, 108, 109, 110, 111, 113, 114(both), 116(tr), 118(l), 119(r), 120, 121(b), 125, 126(t), 127, 132, 138, 139, 140, 141, 142.

PGA World Golf Hall of Fame; pages: 6-7, 72.

St. Andrews University Library, pages: 13, 14(main), 15(t), 44(t), 46(t), 47(r), 64(t), 65(t), 73(both).

Phil Sheldon Golf Picture Library, pages: 40, 42, 49(tl), 52(t), 53(l), 70(br), 71, 78(t), 80, 81(t), 82, 85, 86, 87, 89, 91, 104, 106,-8(both), 115, 122-3, 130, 135, 137(both), 143, 146, 147, 148(both), 157(both).

US Golf Association, pages: 54(b), 68(b).

Volvo Marketing, page: 59.

The author would like to thank John Rollason of Poniente Golf Club, Mallorca, for his invaluable assistance with the instructional part of this book.